Hey!
Is That Guy Dead
Or Is He the Skip...

And Other
Stories
I Wish I'd
Never Written

WILLIAM THOMAS

Illustrations by Tom Banwell

Stoddart

For Monica

Published in 1994 by
Stoddart Publishing Co. Limited
34 Lesmill Road
Toronto, Canada
M3B 2T6
(416) 445-3333
Second printing January 1995

Stoddart Books are available for bulk purchase for sales promotions,
premiums, fundraising, and seminars. For details, contact the
Special Sales Department at the above address.

Canadian Cataloguing in Publication Data
Thomas, William J., 1946-
Hey! Is that guy dead or is he the skip?
ISBN 0-7737-5673-6
1. Curling - Humour. 1. Title.
GV845.T56 1994   796.964'0207   C94-931341-6

Cover Design: Brant Cowie/ArtPlus
Cover Photograph: Grant Ball/Trent Photographic

Printed and bound in Canada

*Stoddart Publishing gratefully acknowledges the support of the Canada
Council, Ontario Ministry of Culture, Tourism, and Recreation, Ontario Arts
Council, and Ontario Publishing Centre in the development of writing and
publishing in Canada.*

Contents

Introduction

These weekly columns, which I've been writing for the last fifteen years, thematically entitled "All the World's a Circus" or "From the Land of the Loony," are considered to be humour columns.

It has always been my intent, with all the sameness and all the sadness dominating the pages of newspapers today, that my column should be a small retreat where the reader can escape for a quick cup of odd. My column is a place where the reader can hide from Bosnian Serbs, economists, and Richard Simmons.

Although I am impressed by the great and famous of this world, I am drawn inextricably to the unusual.

While others might champion Clinton, Gretzky, or Madonna, my kind of Person-of-the-Week is Sherman Hill of San Francisco, who recently became enraged that he should be charged for driving alone in a two-person car pool lane, when the police could clearly see that his seeing-eye dog was right there beside him in the passenger seat. Sherman Hill is totally blind in one eye, partially blind in the other, and claims he needs his seeing-eye dog to alert him to oncoming cars by barking. When Mr. Hill also denied trying to outrun the cops by explaining he was speeding only to cool off his dog, he became a serious candidate for my Man-of-the-Year.

That's just the kind of guys we are, me and Sherman: bent.

And so it was, in March of 1992, when I visited the city of Edmonton, Alberta, on a speaking engagement and wrote a column about some strange goings-on out there.

That column and the reaction to it by people in Edmonton are printed elsewhere in this book. But the upshot of it all was that, having had what I considered some good-natured fun with this western city, you'd have thought that I had called Wayne Gretzky a plug.

Suffice to say, the response by some Edmontonians and the *Sun* newspaper was ugly and quite unexpected. By mail, I was awarded "The Asshole of the Year Award" with my name hand-printed over a Polaroid print of a man's butt. To me it looked like Ralph Klein bending over to pick up a loony in a steam bath, but I could never prove it.

When the flap subsided and people from Edmonton stopped calling me a traitor, an Eastern geek, a wimp, a pig, a puppet, a pauper, a pirate, a pawn, and a king — I realized they'd mistaken me for Frank Sinatra. No, actually I realized it wasn't just people in Edmonton stalking the streets of this country pursuing a pound of flesh — everybody was doing it.

Mordecai Richler writes about his home province, expressing his skewed view that although Quebec is the worst place in the world to live, he could never live anywhere else — and Francophones want his book banned.

Frank magazine runs a tasteless but satirical piece on the deflowering of the daughter of Brian Mulroney, the man largely responsible for our national foul mood, and the prime minister of the most peace-loving nation in the world is quoted as saying he "wanted to take a gun and go down there and do some serious damage" (to the editors).

Under the pressure of the recession, the GST, free trade, native demands, special-interest groups, Francophone demands, Anglophone trade-offs, the jobless, the homeless, the lobbyists, bankruptcies, and the constitutional crisis that's gone on longer than most world wars with no end in sight — under all this self-scrutiny and strain, we are coming apart at the seams.

Seriously, we are losing our sense of humour.

At a time when we need to laugh like never before, we have lost the ability to look at ourselves and be amused by the distorted reflection we see in the glass.

Wrapped tightly in the straitjacket of political correctness, we can hardly make a rude noise, let alone snicker at the sound of one let loose in church.

Two years in a row the United Nations declared Canada to be the best country in the world in which to live, and we're all walking around like nervous sheep on the set of *Silence of the Lambs.*

This country has produced some of the greatest comic minds of our time and, typically, you can see their names listed on the credits of the best comedic material on U.S. television and film.

And what are we producing here as of late? Directives, denouncements, ultimatums, book burnings, subscription cancellations, and gun threats — all to prove we'd rather fight than find something funny.

We now have advertisements on radio put out by the multicultural people telling us what humour can properly be addressed with laughter and what should be scowled at with self-righteous disdain.

As well-intended as such attempts may be — to rightfully rid conversation of racist, sexist, homophobic, and AIDS "jokes" — they have made the Canadian sense of humour a matter of public policy.

What next? Warning labels?

Warning: "This humour column could be fatal when read by thin-skinned, narrow-minded, butt-bound people who haven't laughed since Hurricane Hazel caught the Avon lady coming up the driveway."

Two true stories come to mind when I try to give shape to the quintessential Canadian sense of humour and the importance of maintaining it.

The first story has been documented in several sources but I will paraphrase the account of Beamsville's great Fred C. Dobbs from his book *The Platinum Age of B.S.*

In 1949, Camillien Houde, the mayor of Montreal, visited Calgary as the guest celebrity of a CFL football game between the hometown Stampeders and the Montreal Alouettes. He was to kick off the ceremonial ball.

Quite a character, Houde had been sent to jail by Prime Minister Mackenzie King for urging young men to refuse to join the Canadian Armed Forces during World War II. After the war, he was released and promptly elected mayor of Montreal once more.

So there he was at old Mewata Stadium at centre field with a microphone, surrounded by 15,000 hostile fans screaming things like: "Hey, froggy, how high can you jump?" and "Hey, Houde, how was the crowbar hotel?" and "Hey, Houde, where's your striped suit?" His reception was described as "wicked" and it went on until the mob tired itself out.

Houde waited patiently for silence as he stood with several nervous officials, the game ball on its kickoff tee. Then he said:

"Ladies and gentlemen, I want to tell you that I really have enjoyed my visit with you here. Two days ago they took us out to Banff, and we saw the scenery there and it certainly is more beautiful and more spectacular than anything that we have in the city of Montreal. Yesterday, I was walking around the downtown area and admiring how clean your city is, how orderly it is. And I admired the prettiness of the women of all ages in this city of Calgary, the wonderful expression on their faces, the joy of living that seemed to be there in their smiles. The youthfulness of the West somehow was there. And today, I just can't get over the hospitality shown me here in this stadium. All I can say is that whenever you want me to, I'd be glad to come back out here to kick your balls off!"

The man got a standing ovation.

A little raw, yes, but without a doubt funny, in a uniquely Canadian "gotcha!" kind of way.

If we lose the ability to laugh at and with each other — by region, religion, by race, gender, and language — we diminish what makes this country so world-class special.

Sometimes to a fault, we are the most tolerant and modest people in the world. We leave it to others to tell us how great we are, but we owe it to ourselves to point out our peculiarities and discrepancies. We are at our best in celebration of those family follies in the first official language of this country — laughter.

"Burn the book! Shoot the writer! Take a gun and do some serious harm." By reacting to humorous endeavours which we immediately yet mistakenly deem to be offensive personal attacks, we assuredly chip away at our national soul. The well of tolerance and compassion that Canadians seem to have been blessed with is neither deep nor abiding.

Countries can become cranky old bastards too, drying up and dying, with the spark of life and laughter a mere memory of youth.

Let's hope we've all just been having a real bad day for the last ten years.

Oh yeah, and the second story which defines the fundamental Canadian sense of humour involves me, two ducks, and the game of curling.

I

Curling: The Game for the Nineties
— But You Gotta Be That Old to Enjoy It

Origins

By all accounts, the game of curling began in the early 1600s in England when a church vicar by the name of Sethwick Rearse created a recreational diversion to break up the boredom of rural life in and around Shaftesbury-on-the-Stilton, at Gerfall-by-the-Fife-and-Drum, near Haslemere. When other like-minded vicars of the Church of England visited him, Sethwick Rearse would lead them down into the darkened church basement and engage them in a very rudimentary version of the game, well out of the sight of women and children because even then this sport was deemed to be morally corrupt.

Once there, the men would form a circle, known as the "house," or "vicar's house," and one by one they would drop their trousers and whip one another about the bare buttocks with broom handles.

Quite often the winner would be the man, or in the case of a well-attended tournament, the team that received the worst whipping (or best whoopin', if you know what I mean) in the course of a ten-end match. Sometimes gags were used to stifle the screams of . . . oh, I'm sorry. I was reading from the wrong page of the *History of Sport* — actually that's how *caning* got started.

I apologize for that. It's just that they're so close together, in the index I mean.

In tracing the origins of curling, at least one expert believed that curling was played in the Ice Age, logically deducing that wherever there was ice on earth, there was some sort of game being played on ice.

Another researcher placed the beginning of the game in the Stone Age — hairy monsters, draped in skins, grunting and hurling boulders along the ice into each other's caves or "houses." When markers were set up at the mouths of the caves, the researchers claimed, curling in its most primitive form was created. Recent attempts by experts in Red Deer, Alberta, to establish a genetic link between the Ice-Age hairy monsters and the Russ Howard rink of Penetanguishene, Ontario, have been unsuccessful.

One historian compiled early evidence that brought him to the very compelling conclusion that curling began as a pest war in which large flat metal stones were first used as weapons to kill ice mites. He has since been relieved of his duties at the History of Sport and War Museum at the University of Glasgow at Paisley Preen on Loch Lomond near The-Heather-on-the-Teather, By-the-Deep-Blue-Sea.

While some historians believe curling emerged as a sport sometime in the sixteenth century in the so-called Low Countries, specifically the Netherlands and the tiny protectorate of Flem (pronounced *Phlegm*), the Dutch of today have steadfastly stuck to the statement: "Oh yeah, well you just try and prove it!" When asked about curling, the Flemish look down, clear their throats, and point north towards the Netherlands.

Therefore, historians have focused primarily on Scotland and, to save time, have documented the same date, sometime in the sixteenth century.

The Scottish Highlanders were already famous for sports that featured feats of strength and endurance like caber tossing, shot putting, and hammer throwing, so sports historians are unanimous in their opinions that these same Scots screwed up big time when it came to curling.

In winter, in Scotland, then as now, frosty and wet North Sea winds whipped across the Highlands causing even the toughest of the kilted Scots to wear underwear, a practice most nations of the world had made a habit of doing a century before during the Great Infestation of Cooties. These bone-chilling salty gales would gild the tarns and the lochs of the Scottish hillsides, and since few men knew what a tarn was, they would congregate at the river's edge to drink unblended whisky and skip stones across the water. One day two Scots named Angus and Deeter were skipping stones when the river suddenly froze over. To these pioneers of frozen water sports, this quick freezing meant two things — they too would have to start wearing underwear, and the stones went a lot farther when skipped across ice.

And every day after that, they would venture down to the river's frozen banks, though the wool of their new underwear was giving them both one helluva rash. They tested their weight on the thickening surface and when they deemed it safe, they ventured onto the middle of the river where the ice was smooth and glossy. They brought with them stones, stones ten times bigger than the skipping stones.

Angus, as if by predestination, carved small circles on the surface to be used as targets for the stones. Deeter, following Angus's orders, then threw the stones exactly onto those circles, sending the rocks to the bottom of the river, leaving large gaping holes in the ice. And on that day, oh I don't know, let's say December 17, 1510, late in the afternoon, with the sun going down and 43%-by-volume malt liquor coursing through their veins, Angus and his pal Deeter invented ice fishing (see "Ice Fishing — Guys Watching Bobbers Not Bob," Section IV).

And so it was that caning and ice fishing enjoyed an unparalleled burst of popularity among English and Scottish men of the sixteenth century, and some even enjoyed both sports simultaneously, what with some kilted Scots still holding out on the conversion to underwear and thus being pretty much always dressed for either occasion. It was thus left to real men — men who didn't have the stomach for caning (despite being told many times they were facing the wrong way) and men who found ice fishing too action-packed — to invent the sport of curling.

The earliest known curling stones, also called "channel stanes," "kuting" stones, or "loofies" (shaped like a Scottish "loof," or palm of the hand), had grooves for fingers and a thumb. At first they were thrown through the air to the ice like a bowling ball and also given a bit of a spin or side action. Fortunately, sports historians of the day weren't paying attention and the world was spared the invention of bowling until the seventeenth century by the Dutch — who categorically deny this as well.

The single oldest surviving curling stone is the Stirling Rock, inscribed "St. Js. Stirling 1511." Engraved on the underside of the rock are the words "A Gift" which proves once again that the Scottish Highlanders were really easy to buy for.

The Stirling Rock and two other ancient curling stones, one somewhat triangular and the other oblong, are today on display at the Smith Institute at Dornoch-on-Spey, In-the-Milton-Bog, By-the-Kirk-on-Perth, Along-the-Dee-Dyke-on-a-Wee-Bike.

Mr. James Sword, curator of the Smith Institute, is quoted in Robin Welsh's *Beginner's Guide to Curling* as saying: " . . . the stones attract curlers from many parts of the world and they gaze earnestly through the glass case at the end of their pilgrimage."

One can only assume these stone-gazers from many parts of the world get a real break on airline tickets since they travel within the confines of closed caskets.

Official recognition was given the modern game of curling in Scotland when the Grand Caledonian Curling Club, formed in 1838, was bestowed the blessings of Queen Victoria in 1842. Henceforth, the Royal Caledonian Curling Club became the "mother" club to all curlers. Even today, especially when the skip throws the first rock of a match straight through the house, he will, out loud, pay homage to this "mother" of all clubs.

It was no mere coincidence that Queen Victoria would champion the sport of curling. The Victorian Age was noted for its dim view of real fun and its advocation of sexual abstinence. Even now, wives of avid curlers feel the on-ice sport has replaced anything similar in the bedroom.

In conclusion, it matters little who actually invented curling. In fact it evolved to its modern state in the country of Scotland — they refined it, they regulated it, and they nurtured the game. They also exported it to many, many countries. No doubt about it, the blame is all theirs.

Has the sport changed much since its official arrival on the sports scene in 1842? Not at all. For even then curling was illegal on the Sabbath, and last year CTV dropped its Sunday coverage of the finals of the World Curling Championships in Oberstdorf, Germany.

So you see, the more things change, like heaving "loofies" in your "woollies," the worse that rash will get.

The Game

If I described to you a place in this world where people wearing funny things on their heads stood around throwing rocks into houses, you'd probably guess it was an occupied territory in the Mideast or a disputed town in the Balkans.

But no, that place would be Canada, and the sport would be curling.

After the fall of Quebec City in 1759 and the deaths of Generals Wolfe and Montcalm, the 78th Fraser Highland Regiment soldiers spent their leisure time melting down cannon balls and shaping them into curling stones. In retrospect, these soldiers should surely have been tried for treason. Never mind the wanton destruction of military property, they introduced the game of curling to Canada, for godsakes!

Nonetheless, the first games of curling were played on Quebec's St. Charles River in 1760, and as far as the last games of curling are concerned, well, unfortunately, there's just no end in sight.

Early on, the game of curling was termed the "roarin' game" by a young, enthusiastic Scot. It was later learned that this was not a reference to the noise made by the stones reverberating across the ice, but the reaction of the crowd to his attire. (Moths are hell on natural wool kilts.)

A Concise History of Sport in Canada describes curling as "Canada's oldest and most consistent sport." Wow! Even a flattering plug from a trusted ally makes it sound no better than a really reliable laxative.

Is curling a sport? If you can imagine chess played under really adverse weather conditions with the rook and pawns yelling: "Harrrrrr!", "Noooooo!", and "Sweeeep!", then yes, it is a sport. It's kind of like the shot put on ice. Crokinole with brooms.

Curling is almost identical to bar-room shuffleboard if you take the shuffleboard table into the back walk-in freezer and then play on the floor without the table.

Basically, curling is bowling in which some sick individual has Mazola-oiled the lanes. It's like lawn darts, but not nearly as risky.

Imagine, if you will, street hockey in northern Iceland. Replace the sticks and balls with brooms and stones and essentially you have a lot of guys in balaclavas shouting "Greneckkenvern!" which is Icelandic for "What the —— is going on here?"

So that's curling — a game that requires the following equipment: hat, sweater, baggy pants, non-riding underwear, shoes, and a broom. Replace the broom with a scoop and, generally speaking, it's the same equipment you need to walk a dog on a cool day.

Call it a coincidence, but in the game of curling, the guy who shouts the most and orders people around is always named Skip. His helpers are often, but not always, named Tip, Zippy, and Biff. Oddly enough, women bosses or captains are also named Skip, but more about that in my next book, *Transsexual Curlers — Hey! Who's Got the Shot Rocks Now?!*

Women really like — no, make that love and cherish — curling because for the first time since the invention of the corn broom by George Frederick Handel (there's a cute line in one of his songs, I believe it's from the *Messiah*, in which he sings "leave it to Handel to come up with the corn broom"), for the first time ever, women have the delicious opportunity to see guys sweeping. Oh sure, the men are yelling and screaming and bitching and complaining, but they're bent over sweeping their protruding little buns off.

Consequently, some women who don't really enjoy mixed curling play the game anyway, just so they can get a closer look.

According to a recent study of popular Canadian recreational activities by a Toronto demographer, curling ranks right near the top of the list, with church activities, needle craft, charitable volunteering, picnicking, darts, gardening, fishing, and sightseeing. Only birdwatching and ballroom dancing are growing faster than curling in this country. Go figure, eh?

Today there are approximately 1.5 million curlers in Canada but . . . hey! hey! get back here! . . . there's no reason to panic, because thanks to well-kept club membership lists, we know who these people are and where they live.

Apparently curling is really catching on with young people, especially youths between the ages of eighteen and twenty-eight. This age group is also known as "Generation X" or "The Lost Generation." Coincidence? You be the judge.

The showcase and peak of prestige of Canadian curling is known as the Brier. Each year 80,000 curlers from coast to coast begin their quest of the Brier, but only forty-eight of them end up representing the ten provinces and two territories at the grand championship. And in the end, only the four *crème de la crème* curlers will drink from the $50,000 gold Labatt Tankard, the symbol of excellence of the sport.

The Brier was established in Canada in 1925, when Sir Rodney Oakes was commissioned to study the sport of curling and come up with one thing, one key ingredient that would make the game more aggressive, yet more fun and, above all, more attractive to average Canadians. After six months and two Sports Canada funding grants, Sir Rodney submitted his proposal — a two-word fulfilment of the fundamental Canadian dream: *Labatt's beer*.

As a result of an unfortunate typographical error, the Canadian Curling Association established the Labatt Brier as a symbol of curling supremacy that has flourished to this day. (Sir Rodney was a little pissed off, but if it works, don't fix it, eh?)

To keep Sir Rodney from committing suicide, they put two handles on the golden beer stein, so even he could drink from it.

Today, in descending order of importance, the highest rewards a Canadian curler can receive for his or her relentless efforts at the rink are: a Purple Heart, the Brier Tankard, a Silver Broom, and a new liver.

In *The Name of the Game*, a definitive booklet on the game, its origins, history, and championships, the full-colour centrefold is dedicated entirely to the recipes of six super curling cocktails including Gordon's Keen Ice, Haig's Shot Rock, and the Golden Wedding Runner.

And that's why I love curling and curlers — they put the real objectives of the game right up front and in Black & White where everybody can see them. Curling may be their sport, but partying is definitely their profession.

The Rules

Following are the rules of international play as agreed to by all member countries of the International Curling Federation, who have painstakingly integrated their basic philosophies and amalgamated their rigid structures to create a viable system of official on-ice conduct legally amended by subsequent ICF meetings as to rules 9(3) through 21(2) and 10 (in its entirety) with further jurisdiction reserved for the agreed-upon constitution of revisions zzz . . . zzzzzzz . . .

Oh, sorry. Right. The rules of curling.

Rule #1: Ice is all-important. If ice is unavailable, at least keep the glasses in the freezer before pouring.

Rule #2: Brooms are not to be used as weapons on the ice. At home, however, between two consenting adults . . . (see Origins, caning).

Rule #3:   The sliding delivery may be used by the stone thrower and the waiter bringing drinks to the rink area, but not both simultaneously.

Rule #4:   Intimidating, criticizing, or ridiculing an opponent will not be tolerated except during the annual East-West national classic known as the Brier.

Rule #5:   The curling broom may only be used to clear the stone's path, to clean the underside of the stone, and to rid the opposing skip of dandruff.

Rule #6:   Any right-handed player delivering from the hack on the left side of the centre-line will be given a breathalyzer.

Rule #7:   It is illegal to cut air vents in the back of kilts worn by competitors from out of town.

Rule #8:   A player may remove stones while a game is still in progress only if those stones are lodged in his partner's kidney.

Rule #9:   If a player deviates twice from the proper rotation, the other players may vote unanimously to have him chug-a-lug his beer as well as buy the next round.

Rule #10: Inwicking, the inter-familia reproduction practices in the Outer Hebrides, is no longer sanctioned by the International Curling Association.

Rule #11: That area between the hog line and the tee line is reserved for swines who golf.

Rule #12:   The increased offence and physical exertion created by the new Free Guard Zone now require players to give special attention to the Right Guard Zones.

Rule #13:   The "turn" or "elbow in/elbow out" may be used to indicate the rotation of the stone and at Italian weddings while doing the chicken dance.

Rule #14:   Glassy-eyed competitors mistaking the hack line for the hork line shall be removed from the ice immediately, two sheets to the wind.

Rule #15:   Wives of losing skips may not go "Na, na, na, na, na . . . na!" while the player is still in possession of his broom.

An actual rule, framed on the wall of Scotland's Peebles Club in 1821, states: "When a member falls and is hurt, the rest shall not laugh but render him every assistance to enable him to regain his former erect position." Honest, I'm not making that one up.

Essentially the game of curling consists of you throwing your rocks into a house, then your opponent throws a rock at your rock, rocks hit rocks, some rocks are taken out, and at the end of an end, everybody gets their rocks off, and then they start all over again. It's a very social sport.

Precision timing is not what you'd call essential in curling. Whereas most sports have adopted the Lynx photo-timing system to clock events, curlers have steadfastly stuck with the egg-timer.

There are leads and seconds and thirds and skips and mates and vice-skips and vice-grips and people like that who throw, sweep, and yell, depending upon how they feel that day. Certain players can yell at other players while skips can yell at everybody. A lead can be yelled at by everybody, including spectators in the first four rows. On the grand scale of importance, a lead curler lives on the ground level of a two-storey outhouse, and he's not allowed to wear a helmet.

If your team has more stones nearest a button on the ice, at the end of an end, you win the button . . . sorry, you win that end. After eight or ten ends (nobody's sure), you might win enough ends to win the game.

In the case of a tie, you go into overtime, and the team that remains on the ice after the bartender yells "Last call!" is awarded the match. If you win enough matches at your club, and then go on to win a lot of matches in your local zone and then your region and then your province and then your country — they send you to some obscure place like Oberstdorf, Germany, and once you and your team have cleared Canadian airspace, they cancel TV coverage of your event. At least that's what happened in 1994.

Curling on TV

I once wrote a column on curling stating that I didn't really mind the game as long as it was being played in private covered rinks in remote areas like New Brunswick where children were not exposed to it. Then TSN decided to televise curling live and I, as a viewer of physically active sports, snapped. Among other things, I said that watching curling live on television was like watching postal workers on Valium. *Slow* was the word that first came to mind. My first reaction to TSN coverage was that if curling was a sport, their target audience must be store mannequins and park monuments.

But hey, I was only kidding!

Apparently CFTO, Toronto's CTV affiliate, was not kidding when they decided to drop the World Curling Championships in Oberstdorf, running a movie instead.

Although CTV aired the final on their other affiliates, the Toronto station refused to show the last day of competition, even though Canada had gone all the way, in both the women's and men's events, with the Sandra Peterson rink from Saskatchewan and the Rick Folk rink from British Columbia.

CFTO claimed it was not the sport but the difficulty in convincing advertisers to buy the commercial spots. You can sure see where a gentle and gentlemanly game like curling might be a tough sell in a town where all the available advertising spots are occupied by a raving, ridiculously dressed lunatic and his ill-tempered bull terrier.

And did CFTO replace the world curling finals with something starring a slathering Arnold Schwarzenegger or a burning Bruce Willis or a badly beaten-up Sylvester Stallone, something an action-starved sports audience would suck up and belch over? Not exactly. They aired Perry Mason's *The Case of the Skin-Deep Scandal,* which of course starred Don Cherry, Blue, and a mislabelled tube of flea shampoo and conditioner.

Here, then, is that list, the top ten program choices CFTO placed ahead of curling in audience and advertiser interest:

#1 — Old people having a little difficulty breathing.

#2 — A test pattern with the CFTO logo in the middle.

#3 — Live coverage of the spot where the *Edmund Fitzgerald* went down.

#4 — A Raymond Burr retrospective.

#5 — *Mud Wrestle Mania* with Senator Pat Carney.

#6 — Colour slides of an amateur birdwatcher.

#7 — *Catch and Release,* a Parole Board of Canada film.

#8 — *Celebrity Tractor Pull* with Lloyd Robertson.

#9 — Brian and Mila's *Wave Goodbye to the World* tour.

#10 — *Ebony and Ivory*: Oscar Peterson and Bob Rae play chopsticks.

Great Moments in Curling

In April 1994, at the Canadian Junior Women's Championship in Truro, Nova Scotia, the skip of the Manitoba team poked herself in the eye with the knob of her broom. This was the only recorded injury in the history of curling occurring outside a ten-metre radius of the bar.

For twenty-nine years, the junior men's team from Manitoba could not win the national title. Finally, when they accomplished it in 1979, the skip was a guy named Mert.

To settle the age-old question of curlers — which is faster, the man or the stone? — sweep Larry Fransden once raced a rock. Although the stone was given a mighty heave, it slowed near the hog line where it was passed by the curler. Larry Fransden later passed a sobriety test, but the stone was subsequently disqualified for using a performance-enhancing chemical known as WD-40.

In 1986 at the Brier in Kitchener, Ontario, Prime Minister Brian Mulroney helped the Ed Werenich rink launch the ceremonial opening rock. The Werenich rink was subsequently penalized for having too many hacks on the ice at one time.

In April 1994, a published report heralded the first-ever nude curling bonspiel to be held in Quebec City. The much anticipated event was to include a sightseeing tour and a wienie roast. (Separate events.) Unfortunately, the dateline was April 1 and the report a figment of curling writer Bob Weeks's overworked imagination. Once the hoax was discovered, CFTO decided not to televise the event and instead ran the movie *Buck-naked Fly Fishing with Lloyd Robertson* in its place.

In March 1994, the Canadian Men's Curling Championship was dubbed the Redneck Brier when rude fans began heckling the Russ Howard rink from Penetanguishene, Ontario. The tournament was delayed for four hours when Russ Howard, on the third day of yelling "HARRRRR," blew out the rink's sound system, and hogs, both domestic and wild, began congregating at the front door. It was later determined that the hogs were disgruntled and horny escapees from a Swine Artificial Insemination Centre. (See "Edmonton — Thick Steaks and Thin Skins," Section II.)

In 1986 in Regina, skip Raymond Arnott, while swishing his broom back and forth in front of a rock to indicate a take-out, and with his hand on his hip to indicate an out-turn, was proposed to by a guy named Ross Beard.

In a World Cup match in 1979, New Zealand beat Australia in a game that took four days to play. New Zealand eventually emerged victorious when, after scoring fifty-two consecutive runs on a century stand by the wicket tender who . . . sorry, wrong sport.

In 1989, at the Saskatoon Labatt Brier, a Canadian record was established when 150,000 people passed through the turnstiles for the eight-day event. A second record was set when 149,992 people kept right on going out the back door. Seven people were found hiding in the washrooms. Mrs. Ed Werenich attended every event.

In 1969, Canadian Ron Northcott beat Norway's Erik Gyllenhammer 28-2. This set a curling record for highest total games scored (30), the highest score by one team (28), and the worst whipping ever suffered by a guy named Gyllenhammer (Erik).

In 1977, Carl Gustaf XVI became the first sovereign to attend the World Curling Championships at Karlstad, Sweden. He was also the last.

In 1992, Fruit of the Loom became the official supplier of the Canadian Curling Association, posing a difficult question for the 1993 and 1994 world champion Sandra Peterson rink: Will that be briefs or boxers, ladies?

In the 1993-94 edition of *Curling Canada*, Canadian Airlines ran a full-page colour ad boasting "We Carry More Athletes than TSN." Curlers, objecting to the favouritism shown athletes, demanded equal time.

The Fifteen Most Misunderstood Curling Expressions

Bonspiel   From the French *bon,* or good, and the German *spiel,* or spew. Literally, it means "good hork-up!"

Take-out   A crucial point in a bonspiel where the curlers have to decide between pizza or Chinese food.

Skip   The real name of a guy you'd never want to go camping with.

Third   Pronounced "turd" in French and pertaining to a curler consistently making bad shots.

Biter   A nasty little bugger, usually the skip's youngest child.

Pebbles   The youngest kid on *The Flintstones*.

Coming Home A critical declaration usually made by the bartender: "No, honest, Barb, he's not here, he's *coming home!*"

The Brier Immortalized by Johnny Horton when he sang "they ran through the Brier, and they ran through the brambles, they ran through the bushes, where a rabbit wouldn't go," the story of British soldiers curling while in retreat.

Back-boreds Spectators way in the back who are really bored.

Dead Weight A skip with no pulse, who's still in the game.

"Close a Port" Along with "Open a sherry," words curlers live by.

Wobbler A guy who started early in the day and is just barely hanging in there.

Peels A light beer curlers smuggle in from the States.

Well-laid (Wouldn't touch it with a ten-foot curling broom.)

Crowd-pleasing A phrase seldom heard in this sport.

The Crapshoot Bonspiel

In the end, curlers always get their critics.

I thought I felt the wrath of the Wild West in the fallout from my column on Edmonton. That was before I wrote a column on the game of curling.

One editor who ran the piece dropped my column for good after receiving letters, phone calls, and a threat by a female curler to throw a stone, specifically a curling stone, through the window of the newspaper. I not only received copies of angry letters sent to papers carrying the column, the writers sent copies to their regional, provincial, and national organizations, so that the contempt came in ever-rising waves.

I almost lost my faith in curlers as party people with a balanced sense of humour. And then I got a letter from Gord Dandy of the Welland Curling Club in Welland, Ontario.

Gord was not pleased that I had compared curling on television to watching sedated postal workers. Gord understood that I had not actually described curling as a dull game, but he did make note that I had said it was the only sport you could play while still hooked up to a life-support system.

Gord acknowledged that I had never actually referred to curling as a simple game, but he did remember I had said it was the sport Joe Clark planned to take up . . . after he *expired*. I meant *retired*, Gord. Honest.

Gord Dandy, like all the others, had missed the point of the column.

All I said was that curling as we know it should either be banned outright or restricted to unlit "ice" houses in northern New Brunswick and played by people who are bonded and have fixed abodes. That or change it. Slightly. I believed that a little more action wouldn't hurt — like legal bodychecking, boarding, tripping, tackling from behind, and, above all, "high brooming."

I also thought scoring would be more interesting if the guy who threw the rock had to hold onto it all the way to the centre of the house, as the other team tried to kick it and beat it out of his hands.

Going with some of my suggested changes, I had a curling scene in that column that involved pushing, shoving, a fight between players, and a lounge-clearing brawl. It was great — women slapping each other with their tams, men lifting their kilts and mooning innocent bystanders, a skip whose name really was Skip getting crushed by a Zamboni — it was crude, crazy, and very Canadian. It was *Curling Night in Canada* with Don Cherry as your host.

And that's where Gord Dandy and the Welland curlers got their rocks in the wrong house. My point was, let's take the violence out of hockey and put it in curling, a sport that desperately needs it.

But Gord Dandy did something very different, something rudely beautiful. He sent me a letter inviting me to a new event at the Welland Curling Club — The William Thomas Crapshoot Bonspiel.

Essentially, in honour of my curling column, they would organize a special event in which thirty-two of my columns would be placed on the curling rink face-up and numbered. Around this display of my life's work would be built a pen. He estimated about a hundred or so enthusiastic members would watch from the upstairs lounge as two plump domesticated ducks, who had recently eaten a lot, would be placed in the pen.

The natural bodily functions of these two waddling birds would then provide the remainder of the evening's entertainment.

The curler holding the number of the column most visibly destroyed by the ducks would win the grand prize of the bonspiel. A special bonus prize would be awarded to the curler holding the number of the column on which my photograph at the top had received special attention from the fluffy ends of the ducks. "A direct hit or two" was the way Gord characterized it. It was what curlers everywhere wanted to do, but in the interest of public decency, they hired two ducks to do the job.

And he was most gracious in inviting me. He said they didn't know any real celebrities, so would I like to come down and make an appearance at the event.

And I did! I really did!

I have to be honest — I actually curled and I loved it. Yeah, Gord and the gang even let me be the lead rock, almost every end. After about three hours I asked them to spin me to the left for a while because I'd lost all feeling on my right side.

Then a very sweet lady taped my foot with Scotch tape so "it would slide better" when I was sweeping. Unfortunately, she taped the wrong foot, and on my first trip chasing a rock down the ice, I had to stop myself by crashing through the end of the rink.

Then, after the curling, they brought out the ducks — fat, irritable, and fully corked. I'm not making this up. Before they put them in the pen, Gord pooped . . . sorry, popped . . . the corks from the back ends of the birds.

And I was struck dumb. So I asked the mayor of Welland, Dick Reuter, who looked like a farmer to me, if this was actually possible, to cork a bird. Dick said, oh sure, he and his wife Bonna used to do it all the time on long car trips with the kids. The city of Welland and Mayor Dick seemed like a perfect fit.

Once the prize winners were declared and all my columns were covered in a greenish slime, the real fun began. A curler by the name of Delwin Fraipont (I'm serious) introduced me by saying some very nice things about my columns. Mainly he said they were very absorbent.

33

It must have been about ten o'clock when I got up to speak. Somewhere around eleven o'clock, when the booing subsided, I spoke.

I thanked the curlers for honouring me with this event and for showing me how to curl. It was then that I publicly dubbed curling "the game for the nineties." Then, switching off the microphone, I whispered in the mayor's ear: "But you gotta be that old to enjoy it!"

Dick said, "Huh?", so I knew I was onto something here.

Now I didn't actually cry, not like I did when the ducks gave my columns a dung dip in the pen, but I did get a little emotional.

For Gord Dandy and the Welland crowd had responded to my critique on curling the way we, as Canadians, used to have fun with each other. For a moment, alone at the microphone, with the ducks in the background quacking for fresh columns, I saw a ray of laughter and light penetrate the ugly mood that's covered us all in this country for this past difficult decade.

The trouble with characters like Camillien Houde and Gord Dandy is there just aren't enough of them in Canada.

And that's why I now love curling — the people. Curlers are fun — they party like it's part of the sport, and they're able to laugh with and at each other. Plus, they're starting to take my advice. I mean any time you introduce two defecating ducks into the game of curling, by my calculations you easily increase the excitement level by seventy-five percent!

I love this game, I really do. "Spin me the other way, Gordo, I think I'm going to hurl!"

II

Four Countries and a City
I Can Never Go Back To

Japan – Ohio Buckeye Country

In the summer of 1991, I toured Japan with a Canadian basketball team, a very good intermediate squad of mostly former university stars now playing in the Niagara peninsula. The name of the team was POITS, an acronym for that catch-all Canadian saying: "Piss On It, Tomorrow's Saturday!"

Japan is the complete conundrum, the Pandora's box of the Pacific, which can confound the most sophisticated world traveller. You can only imagine what it does to guys who, up to this point in their lives, have made it a rule never to venture more than sixty miles away from their local Beer Store.

Pat Rosinski, a forward from Fenwick with the Niagara POITS basketball team, was the first of us to be confused.

"Duty free?" Pat asked the oriental woman at the airport information booth. Then using a lot of hand and body language to shape a bottle and pretending to drink it, he repeated: "Duty free?"

It took another POITS member, Pat's brother Mark, to remind him that he didn't need the loud enunciation or hand gestures, since we were merely changing planes at the Vancouver airport and pretty much still on Canadian soil.

That's just what a confounding country Japan is — it can mess you up a full fourteen hours before you get there.

Suffice to say that, while Portugal is similar to Spain and Chile might remind you of Argentina, Japan is a lot like Saturn.

But I've always considered myself a *vive la différence* kind of guy, and there's no better place in the world to experience the extreme variation of custom than a totally automated, electronically controlled country like Japan, where people still sleep on the floor and eat food with sticks.

It's a little like watching R2D2 beat his laundry on rocks down by the river's edge.

Staring into their front yards, which are actually in-ground goldfish bowls, you realize almost immediately that Japan is definitely a carp of a different colour.

But, of course, I'm isolating only those things odd to an occidental tourist, because the truth is the Japanese are the most gracious and generous hosts on the face of the earth and the mere mention of an item means it will be found, bought, wrapped, and in your suitcase before you leave for the airport. Hence, a good word to avoid in Japan is *koi* (carp).

Being billeted at a "homestay" or Japanese family in Kanazawa was, for me, the highlight of the trip.

Normally, spending time with ordinary Japanese people would be infinitely interesting, except that I spent a lot of time with Dale Hajdu, POITS captain, my roommate, my accountant. In Japanese, this is known as *chotto-matti* — punishment for having been mean to a bunny rabbit in a previous life.

So Dale and I spent four days and nights living with a boy named Su, something rare indeed for guys who like girls and are not that fond of Johnny Cash.

Tsuda Yashushi, a graceful athlete on the All-Ishikawa Prefectural Team, picked us up at the train station where television crews and print reporters covered the arrival of the Canadian team like an Olympic event. What a country, we thought.

Su had a remote control in his car so you could operate the CD player from the back seat.

We went immediately to his house in a small suburb of Kanazawa, where he took us into a tiny room and explained in the best international language of hand signals and blank stares that no, this was not where we would store our luggage. The luggage must go outside because this was our bedroom. Two mats side-by-side on the floor represented our double bed. "What a sense of humour!" we said.

Now I'm not above bribing an accountant for a better tax return, but if anybody had ever suggested I would one day sleep with mine, I'd have crammed a bunch of T-4 slips up his nose.

On the trip to Kanazawa, as honoured guests of the tour's sponsor, the Hokeotsu Bank of Nagnoka, we had been approached at every juncture of the bullet-train trip from Tokyo by company employees who ceremoniously presented each of us with cold beer and lunch packs. This happened at least four times in ten hours.

Now here we were, sitting cross-legged at the dining table of a guy named Su, having just tied our suitcases to his roof and not having slept for nearly two days, when our host emerged from the kitchen with a beautiful ornate tray of . . . cold beer and lunch packs.

We said *"domo arigato"* and said "what a country!" but it just didn't have the same zip to it as the first half-dozen times.

Then Su pointed out a blue label on the side of the small metal keg of beer that read in English "Cold and Ready to Drink." We thought that was fine until, right before our bleary eyes, the blue label slowly disappeared. I said that's it, I'd had enough beer for today. But then Su explained that the metal tankard of Sapporo Beer was temperature controlled with the label automatically disappearing when the beer dropped below an acceptable temperature.

Then Su pressed a button, and the movie *Cannonball Run* came on television in Japanese; he pressed another button and, as the Japanese dialogue faded, the English sound track emerged. A place where beer tells you when to drink it and the television talks to you in two languages. What a country!

And just before we all dived into the sushi and cold shrimp with our *hashi* (chopsticks) and toes (toes), Su said: "Grass?"

And I said: "Grass?"

And Dale said: "Grass?"

And Su rose immediately and went out to the kitchen to get the stash, and we both said: "What a country!" Cold beer, exotic food, and now he wants us to smoke some dope?

When Su returned from the kitchen with *glasses* for the beer, Dale and I were noticeably relieved. We'd spent the whole time ripping through the Japanese dictionary for the term "bail bond."

It's just this kind of confusion that has prompted me to put together a ten-tip guide for people travelling to Japan for the first time.

For instance, if you travel with a basketball team utilizing a man-to-man defence, shouting "Okay I got the short guy!" is very bad strategy.

TIP #1: Don't say that.

Contrary to what Canadians believe, not everybody in Japan is the size of Larry Grossman. Their basketball players are all more than six-feet tall, some exceptionally so. Their problem is the lack of weight and strength.

It's only my own theory, but I believe a Japanese athlete cannot maintain a lot of body weight by eating foods which are still alive at the point of entry, and can therefore swim quickly through the digestive tract before any calories or nutrition can be extracted from them.

TIP #2: No matter how frustrated you get, never say: "Seriously, would it kill you to cook some of this stuff?"

You must understand that the Japanese, a fabulously hospitable race of people, simply prefer a different diet than most Canadians. They routinely serve an array of delicacies we see mostly in jars at veterinary clinics and Rusty's Bait & Tackle.

For example, a Canadian will remove seaweed from his boat propeller, curse at it, and then throw it away. A Japanese will wrap it around rice and eat it like a Tim Horton TimBit. So it's not as if we don't have Japanese food in this country. It just never occurred to us to eat it.

In Canada, raw salmon eggs are great if you're trolling for muskie; in Japan, they're served for breakfast with a light soy sauce.

Then there are *uragiyas*, country restaurants beside rivers where the very popular national dish of *uragi* is served. *Uragi* is grilled over barbecues and served over rice and is very, very tasty until it is translated into English. Then it's eel. Deep down, eel is — as every Canadian knows — actually a snake that is really good at holding its breath under water.

Eating the roasted heads of *uragi* is said to be very lucky in Japan. Getting out of there without blowing lunch all over my *happi* coat did indeed make me feel pretty fortunate.

The bottom line is, our diets are different. What we would normally call in a professional exterminator for, the Japanese will serve up as a side dish on a bed of mountain fern. Nonetheless, they are thinner, healthier, and live longer than we do.

41

TIP #3: Next time, think hors d'oeuvres before you call Abell Waco.

The common misconception concerning habits of imbibing is that Canadians are big drinkers and the Japanese are modest drinkers. The truth is that Canadians are big drinkers and the Japanese are faster and crazier big drinkers.

I saw bank vice-presidents who, minutes after delivering a long and serious speech on Japanese culture, were leading the countdown to a beer chug-a-lug contest.

Japanese men work from eight a.m. to eight p.m., after which two to four hours are dedicated to some of the most suicidal sucking-back of sake, whisky, and beer ever witnessed by a westerner.

TIP #4: Always drink with the Japanese person you can most comfortably carry home.

In Japan, you are forbidden to pour yourself a drink. You must only pour the drinks of the people next to you, and they in turn will pour your drink. Don't get stuck next to a talker; otherwise, you'll spend the entire evening staring at your empty glass.

TIP #5: Never go to Japan with my sister Gail.

On the bright side, however, you cannot become an alcoholic in Japan without somebody else aiding and abetting your excesses.

TIP #6: If you do drink, travel with a sympathetic friend instead of an accountant.

The Japanese never say "no." They have no such word in their vocabulary, but they say *hai* a lot, meaning "yes," and they say it so often and with such enthusiasm that it comes out as a loud, sharp "hike!"

TIP #7: Never travel through Japan with a sports team that lines up in a crouch position, waiting for a ball to be snapped every time somebody says: "Hike! Hike!"

Most toilets in Japan are of the old traditional European type (read: a porcelain hole in the floor), but some are western style and a few are considered space-age technology. One day, you may be fortunate enough to find an ultra-modern commode as I did in a bank manager's office, the kind with a heat-controlled seat and the four-cycle water spout device.

TIP #8: Never hit the rinse button unless you're wearing a raincoat and galoshes.

Some very swank urinals in Japan are electronically operated. That is, a light sensor beam tells the device that the user is at least three feet away and it can now flush itself.

TIP #9: Never get caught gawking with your mouth open as you step back and forth in front of a urinal's sensor beam marvelling at how it flushes automatically. It just looks bad for all of us, eh?

Formal greetings are everything in Japan and, I have to admit, this was not the forte of me and my accountant. Returning to our Kanazawa homestay each day, we could never remember the traditional homecoming salute, but we had determined, after a lot of "Cold and Ready to Drink," that Su's mother worked at a factory making "tuna surprises." (We're still not real sure about this.)

Anyway, each day we would greet her at the door, bow, and say in English: "We hope you had a prosperous day, and that all your tuna were surprised." We're not particularly proud of this but believe me, it was the best that two university-educated Canadians could come up with under the circumstances.

But that wasn't the worst. If you remember nothing else, Tip #10 could someday save your life in Japan.

In Japanese "good morning" is *ohaiyou*, (pronounced "ohio"). I know, I spent a half a morning in a street market arguing about this with vendors. They would point to my red Maple Leaf pin, and I would say: "Canada." And they would appear to understand, but then they would say "ohio." And I would say: "Not Ohio, Canada, Canada — don't you people have atlases?"

Dale, being a big sports fan, automatically added "Buckeye" to the end of "ohio," and every morning for fourteen days we greeted each other with "ohio buckeye." "Ohio buckeye!" was our morning travel slogan for every event, as was "what a country!" for anything that happened past noon.

I can't tell you how hysterical our homestay families would get every time Dale and I would bow to each other and say "ohio buckeye!" On the fifteenth day, Paul Faris, our good friend and tour organizer, who speaks fluent Japanese, took us aside and explained to us that *bakay* (pronounced "buckeye") is a bad word in Japan. Very bad. In fact, for fourteen straight days, Dale and I had come out to have breakfast with each family we stayed with and began by bowing to each other and saying "ohio buckeye" (or in Japanese *ohaiyou bakay)*, meaning, literally: "Good morning, you stupid son-of-a-bitch."

TIP #10: Don't say *ohaiyou bakay* unless you mean it.

Portugal – Last One There's a Rotten Egg

J ust back from a month in Portugal, I would encourage anyone to visit this precious and generous country which makes a foreigner feel like a valued guest, unlike say France, which makes a foreigner feel like he's suspected of poisoning the nation's water supply. Not only are the Portuguese enormously warm and honest, but the best part is, if you order chicken in restaurants, you get to say *frango* a lot.

I have to say that the country of Portugal offers the most boring bullfights in all the world. At least, I thought they did. I must have sat in that cold, damp building for four hours with nothing whatsoever happening until it was explained to me that *corrida* means "bullfight" in Spanish. In Portuguese, *correio* means "post office."

After watching a thousand people drop letters through a slot, I thought if the Portuguese considered this a sport, curling could someday be very big over here.

If you go to Portugal, be clear on this: In Spanish bullfighting, they kill the bull, but in Portugal they only torture the postmaster with a cattle prod.

Everyone should go to Portugal. It's a beautiful and colourful country whose people are honest, placid, and cordial — plus you get to drive like a freakin' maniac and nobody notices.

While I was there, Lisbon made seatbelts compulsory, and if you've ever seen the way taxi drivers tear around that city, you'll know this law will have the same effect as gun control legislation in Bosnia.

No doubt many of us in this country don't always obey the rules of the road, but at least in Canada, we *have* rules of the road!

Driving in Portugal is like the Wild West Show of Europe. After a month behind the wheel of a rental car, I can tell you that there are no highway laws being observed in this nation except for two: one being *ultimo a chegar e um ono mile,* which translates as "last one there's a rotten egg," and two, beep twice and you can do anything your creative and criminal mind desires.

A stop sign in Portugal means take your foot off the accelerator until you're through the intersection. Speed limit signs are strictly adhered to . . . by horse-drawn vehicles and motorcyles with more than one family on board. And a yield sign is like the green flag in racing, it begins the Machismo 500. (Note: A Portuguese man will yield to another driver, but only if the other driver is armed and has his siren on. And then only reluctantly.)

Passing on hills is okay. Passing a car on the right is always a real surprise for the new guy in the rental car. And passing on curves is fine, provided you present your passport upon landing in Spain if you're the operator of the vehicle which careers off the edge and over the 700-foot unmarked, unfenced cliff.

Passing a car a short distance from an oncoming truck is popular and apparently permitted as long as you remember to beep twice.

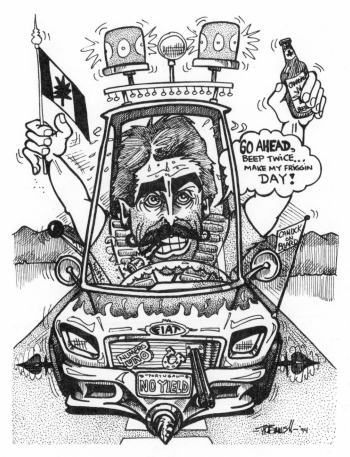

For the tourist in Portugal, "Beep! Beep!" from behind signals the beginning of the chase scene in *Bullitt*.

Upon hearing the horn, you veer to the right shoulder and the passing vehicle screams by on that part of the road we refer to in Canada as the double white line.

I'm making only some of this up. With 2,455 deaths and 70,600 injuries caused by accidents last year alone, Portugal leads Europe in these categories by so much that other countries would have to include possum and raccoons in their statistics just to catch up.

Perennially number one on Europe's highway fatality hit parade, last year Portugal's motor vehicle deaths doubled its nearest contender, Greece, where drivers are described as only "demonically possessed." Per capita, Portugal's road death rate is four times higher than that of the United States.

As you read these statistics, consider also that Portugal is a country without snow and ice.

And all this wouldn't be as bad if most roads were two-lane highways, instead of paved-over ox-paths tiered on the side of mountains.

As far as I could see, *guts* were the only requirements for taking to the road. In Portugal, driver's licence applicants aren't road tested; they just measure how long they can hold their hands over lit candles.

Believe me, Portugal's fastest growing industry is Rescue 911.

And in eight days, I never saw a radar trap or a highway policeman. These guys aren't stupid; they do their job in boats somewhere off shore.

On one wicked bend in the road north of the city of Sagres, I was waved through a construction zone by a flagman who apparently had a lot of trouble distinguishing between the green and red sides of his sign.

Unfortunately, a speeding motorcycle had been waved through by the flagman at the other end. We were headed directly at each other on a single strip of road. He could, of course, have pulled onto the shoulder, but in Portugal this would be a dishonour to the family, most of whom are already mourning other drivers. My only choice was to the right — onto a fresh lane of tar that hadn't yet been rolled.

There we were hurtling at each other like two drivers in the *Joey Chitwood Daredevils Show*. The game was *pollo* (chicken) or, as I prefer to call it, *frango* (spring chicken).

He was a typical Portuguese driver (Randy "the Macho Man" Savage), and I was representing Canada (Scott Goodyear with a face the colour of my little Maple Leaf pin).

I will not dishonour his family or my mother by telling you who won this test of wills. No, I will not tell you who chickened out first. I will, however, tell you that if you rent a black Fiat Uno from Eurocar at the airport in Lisbon, the one with a lot of tar still rattling around in its wheel wells — the shocks are all shot to hell too.

(Another problem of Portuguese drivers is many of them are very short and stocky and can't see over the steering wheel. But not all Portuguese men are short. In fact, some are very tall and muscular, and it's to these guys I prefer you didn't show this story. Thank you.)

So, to make your stay in Portugal more enjoyable, I have compiled a short list of travel suggestions.

Instead of renting a compact car from an airport agency, take a cab to the Portuguese army barracks just north of Lisbon and see if they'll rent you an armoured personnel carrier.

Of course, it is only fitting that as a benign intruder in a foreign country, you at least try to speak the native tongue. That's why in Portugal it's appropriate that you learn a little German. Believe me, when Germany completed its unification program, I had no idea Portugal was included in the deal.

But as I found out, speaking German is really easy if you just make the endings rhyme a little and throw in some official international-sounding words.

Take, for instance, the sentence: "Where is the cutoff for the nude beach, sir?" In my improvised German, this would be something like: "Autoshtoppen . . . knockers floppen . . . knickers droppen, senhor?" Add a clever little pantomime routine to go with the nouns and before you know it, you're ogling two kilos of fresh caught *bacalhau* (cod) at the local Super Mercado.

Now, if by accident you should end up at a nude beach, as I did, there are two things you should know.

First, if an incredibly rude and insensitive person (in Portugal, these are called Frenchmen) begins pointing and laughing at your white parts, quickly dressing so that you can moon him loses something in this particular international situation. Declaring publicly that his mother sleeps with the local squid-fishing fleet is a much more effective response. Remember, most naked guys won't chase you through the nearest town.

Second, when you return to your *pensao*, your sweet little Portuguese landlady will not be impressed by those pressure marks around your eyes left by the binoculars.

Of course, you'll want to engage your hosts in pleasant conversation, and American movies being all the rage in Europe, a good ice-breaker might be: "Hey whaddayathinka Costner's latest flick — Dancing com Lobos?"

I saw "Dancing com Lobos" in Lisbon, and it's really neat to see an American film foreignized. The Portuguese, for instance, have gone with the more traditional ending of this movie in which Kevin Costner's horse *(cavalo)* is chased through the house *(casa)* by *uno naked bandido* (Teddy Kennedy).

Like most Europeans, Portuguese men spit a lot, but thanks to an early-warning system, which begins somewhere south of the navel and rises slowly toward the point of expectoration, you have approximately two minutes to find a bus back to your hotel room before the act is completed.

The Portuguese pride themselves on the abundance and freshness of their fish. Nonetheless, as a Westerner with somewhat different eating habits, you should request and in many cases insist that your *prato depeixe* (fish dish) be served *muito morto* (quite dead).

Despite what they may claim, a sea bass that knocks over your wine glass while trying to get at your shrimp cocktail is most definitely not *muito morto*.

For some strange reason, all the washrooms in Europe offer the visitor a choice of two toilets. It's best to use the one with the seat. If you do use the one without the seat, I'm warning you, don't fiddle with the water faucets.

Many Portuguese words look like their English equivalent, but some are not. I can't tell you the number of times I ordered a *banheira split* and got a tour of the bathroom. Don't be fooled. *Banheira* means "bathtub." The Portuguese word for banana is *Chiquita*; you can tell because the bananas all have little stickers on them.

Occasionally you will need information in English and the best place for this is not Tourism Portugal, but any bar that advertises "English Fish & Chips Sold Here." Inside you will find two-toned people (ghost-white and lobster-red) sitting around bitching about the fact that Portuguese cuisine does not include "mooshy" peas. These are the English, a people who, by law, should be allowed only to read about foreign countries, but never actually to visit them. To avoid a bout of interminable whining, buy them warm beer and introduce them to a Frenchman.

Gusto muito Portugal! I do. I really do.

The Dominican Republic
– If It's Broke, Don't Fix It!

I love the Dominican Republic. The weather is always grand, the people are fantastic, by far the friendliest in all the Caribbean.

The DR is a Third World country where things seldom work, but the people are kind and full of hope. It's like Canada after Mulroney was finished with it.

The Dominican Republic is populated by six million gentle souls and, according to our Toronto tour rep, was founded when "In 1942, Columbus sailed the ocean blue." So it's relatively a young country whose official motto is: "Live Free, or One, Two, Three — Merengue!"

All domestic and personal problems in the Dominican are solved by dancing. On a bad day, this nation is one big conga line from Puerto Plata to Santo Domingo.

After three trips to this country, I have created a Q & A Spanish language course highlighting the most common phrases a visitor to the island might need. Please note that as a world traveller, I have gone beyond the literal meaning to the cryptic message lurking in linear regions of the mind of the messenger. If you get my drift.

For instance, *buenos dias* means "good morning," *por favor* means "please," and *gracias* means "thank you." *El camion esta respaldar encima tu equipaje* means "el truck has backed ojer jer luggage."

Question: *por que*? Translation: But why? Answer: *No se. No se* means "I don't know." But more than any other phrase in the Dominican Republic, *no se* has a multitude of non-literal existential meanings. In this specific case, it translates: "I have no !@#%*! idea."

Question: Why are those guys throwing the luggage over the closed tailgate of the truck and bouncing the pieces off the roof of the cab before they fall to the floor? Answer: *No se.* Translation: Luggage tossing, or the *Samsonite Hammer,* is a demonstration sport in the 1996 Olympics in Atlanta, Georgia.

Question: You call that a luggage truck? Answer: *Si.* Translation: You're lucky Wednesday is not garbage day in the Dominican Republic; otherwise that truck wouldn't be available at all, Mr. Smarty Pants.

Question: Why does it take an average of sixteen baggage handlers to move one piece of luggage through customs and eight guys named Fernando to get you into a taxi? Answer: *Estat nuestra costumbre.* Translation: There are six million people in this country. Forty . . . pardon me . . . fifty-four of them have jobs . . . the rest of us live on tips.

Meanwhile, back at the hotel and six hours later, a question: Where is my luggage that el truck hass backed ojer? Answer: *No se.* Translation: We are working on the theory that a Señora G. Tomaso over at the Jack Tar Village has been delivered your bag by accident.

53

Question: Do you think she'll give my luggage back? Answer: *No se*. Translation: This woman is so souped up on duty-free liquor, she is now playing catch against a wall with your ball and glove, wearing your Cleveland Indians cut-offs, and we can't get near her.

Question: How come I have two refrigerators in my room but no dresser for my clothes? Answer: *No se*. Translation: Look, we are kind of new at this. Up until ten years ago, we were able to keep pleasure-seeking cheapskates like yourself out of our country. We still have a few wrinkles to iron out. Relax. Tomorrow, it will be very hot. Put your clothes in your refrigerators overnight.

Question: How come every day three guys come to my door to check the "Bar-in-Your-Room, Fully Stocked for Your Convenience" refrigerator to see what I've used, and every day I tell them I can't use it because I don't have the key to open it, and every day they say they're coming back with the key, but all they ever come back with is the question of how much did I use from the refrigerator. How come? Answer: *Por que* is always a better way to begin a sentence than *"how come."* Translation: I told you. Relax. Sit back. Put your feet up. Chill out. Have a drink from the "Bar-in-Your-Room, Fully Stocked for Your Convenience" refrigerator.

Question: Is the water okay to drink? Answer: *Si*. Translation: How much did you have and when? Answer: Two glasses, two minutes ago. Order: *Quito el passillo, muy pronto*. Translation: Clear the lobby muy pronto, Pedro, this could get ugly fast!

I couldn't help but notice what with the daily power failures and the daily water shortages that you can't shower, read, flush a toilet, or keep your clothes cold in the refrigerator.

Question: In times like these what is one to do? Answer: Merengue! Clarification? Answer: *Merengue . . . one, two, three merengue . . . it's our musica, our costumbre . . . it's one, two, three merengue!*

Question: How come fifty souvenir shops in a row all sell exactly the same cheap and tacky merchandise? Answer: *No se*. Translation: How do you say in your country, *K-Marta*?

Question: Can you get someone to fix my refrigerator? Answer: *Es tu loco*? Translation: If we had people who could fix refrigerators, do you think we would still be using windmills at the power plant?

Omar Grecco, the international superstar singer no one has ever heard of and whose name is on every marquee on every hotel in Puerto Plata . . . who is this guy anyway? Answer: *No se*. Translation: He is the brother-in-law to Zamfir, master of the pan flute.

I saw a steel manufacturing plant near the airport. Question: What do they make there? Answer: *No se*. Translation: Baseball gloves for George Bell.

Question: Why is it George can't catch a baseball? Answer: *Su madre*. Translation: My uncle is from Santo Domingo and he knows George's mother. She can't catch a baseball either.

Question: Why does everybody go around in golf carts here? Answer: *Menos pollution*. Translation: You wouldn't get into one of our cars would you?

Statement: Last night we were having drinks on my balcony and a beautiful orange and yellow bird flew low over the table and dropped one in my glass of Scotch. Reply: *Como terrible!* Translation: It's a good thing you weren't having dinner.

Everytime there's a problem, people say *mucho jente*. Question: Exactly what does this mean? Answer: *No se*. Translation: Man, there's so much flying by us we can't get a make or model let alone a licence plate number.

Question: Are we having some kind of fun or what? Answer: *One, two, three merengue . . .* hey! hey! hey! *. . . one, two, three merengue!*

There are two fantastic forms of entertainment for tourists in the Dominican Republic: taking in a professional baseball game, and taking a taxi to the stadium and back.

All the hotels in the Dominican have a wide variety of recreational sports like volleyball, snorkelling, tennis, and spot the German tourist who is thin and polite. This game started out as a penny pool among North American tourists at my hotel. When I left, no winner had been declared, and the pot was up to $1.7 million.

On the fringe of every Dominican Republic hotel sits a taxi shack where loud music and napping seem to be the order of the day. It may look like a wrecker's yard and sound like a festival, but it is in fact one of many nerve centres of the island's transportation network.

In the Dominican Republic, you often have to take as many as three taxis to reach your destination because the first two usually break down. *Nerve* is the operative word here. My cab driver's name was Dion and we got along famously, mainly because I made no mention of that ugly incident which caused him to leave the Belmonts.

Dion's shiny red 1972 Sedan Anonymous was a piece of work. Actually, it was a lot of pieces that needed a lot of work. From a distance, it looked like a high school shop project gone berserk. Up close it made you wonder how necessary this trip really was.

The inside door panels were from another car and had been screwed to the interior with the bolts from the outside. Vice-grips served as handles for the windows, and from the front passenger seat, I could see pavement going by under my feet.

But the thing that bothered Dion the most? The radio wasn't working.

Dion had no dashboard in his taxi, which made it easier to jiggle certain wires, thus activating the onboard computer system (turning signals).

I don't know if you've ever seen somebody work on the engine of a car while driving it, but for me, even a day later when I was again able to speak, it was a real thrill.

As a passenger, you could see straight through to the motor, and I think if you're paying good *pesos* for a hired car, it helps justify the price if you get to watch most of the moving parts in action.

We made several stops that afternoon, and each time we had to restart the taxi, Dion would get out, lift the hood, and threaten certain reluctant but vital elements of the engine with a Phillips screwdriver. Then he'd yell "Okay!" and I would turn the ignition key on.

If you ever find yourself in my situation — the switchman on the Dominican Taxi Start-up Team — make sure the automobile is not in gear. The first time I did this, the car lurched forward, and I had a vision of being charged with vehicular manslaughter while still sitting in the passenger seat.

To Dion's credit, he's got a head-first slide that would impress Robbie Alomar.

Returning to the hotel on the coast road, we caught a tail wind and managed to exceed the speed limit by about twenty kilometres. I first spotted the radar sign beside the road and pointed to it. The lady in the back, who was sharing my taxi and my misery, yelled: "Oh, look, radar!"

Dion, still brooding over the fact that I had tried to kill him with his own car, did not respond.

Around the bend, one of three Dominican police officers blew a shrill whistle and waved at the car in front of us to pull over. The car immediately pulled over.

The same cop then whistled and waved at our taxi. The lady poked me, and I looked at Dion who stared straight ahead while maintaining maximum speed.

The cop then jumped onto the road, whistling and waving furiously for us to pull over, and Dion, in a nifty manoeuvre, managed to miss him without once taking his foot off the accelerator.

I covered my face to avoid identification later down at the station, then looked at Dion who waved the whole thing off and explained: *"Mañana."*

Tomorrow? Yeah, but what if they don't ask you to pull over tomorrow? What if tomorrow you're the lead story on the *Dominican Republic's Most Wanted*?

Technically, isn't that like breaking the law? I asked. I turned around in time to see three Dominican policemen, who had been dropped off at the radar trap and therefore were without a chase car or motorcycle, all shaking their fists at us as we sped away.

Either that or they may have just been shaking simbas and doing the *merengue*: *one, two, three merengue!* You're never really sure.

In front of the hotel, as I exited the taxi, the door kind of came off in my hand. As I paid him, Dion explained to me that he needed the money very badly. I wasn't surprised, his bail budget alone must be staggering.

Dion went on to explain he needed money for car repairs. Really? I saw nothing that a good tow truck couldn't take care of. I was very generous. I gave him both a tip and his front right door.

A few days later, I saw Dion sitting in his taxi near the hotel, and I asked him if he'd had the repairs done. He smiled the smile of a man complete and content. Then he shook his head no and punched a button beside the steering wheel. The music came on full blast. The car was still broken, but the radio was working real good.

One, two, three merengue!

Ah, baseball — the last chords of the anthem drowned out by the applause of the crowd, the umpire stooping over to brush off the plate, the silent speed of a fastball shattered by the crack of the bat followed instantly by the hard slap of horsehide on leather as a line-drive double dies in the infielder's glove over second base and a large black duck rises in right field where it has been eating fresh grass clippings. The duck begins to lazily circle the ball field.

The fans go into a frenzy, throwing empty rum bottles, hats, and shoes at it. The duck, struggling to achieve enough altitude to escape the stadium, must make a second circuit around the field, and this time the players from both teams come out of the dugouts to throw gloves and balls and bats at the bird. A drunken fan along the left-field bleachers runs down several steps to throw a flagpole spear-like at the duck and falls face first onto the concrete walkway.

In a last-ditch effort to escape, the duck soars upward over the *Presidente Beer* billboard in left centre field and clears it — only to slam awkwardly into the *Don Pedro's Linea Exclusiva De*

Embutidos sign behind it. The duck gracelessly falls down between the two advertising boards and disappears.

I was there to write and co-produce a film on minor league baseball entitled *Chasing the Dream*. I turned to the sports reporter sitting beside me in the press box and asked: "What would they do if they caught him?"

"They keel heem and heet heem," he replied. "It ees tradition."

Thank God, I thought, that the San Diego Chicken doesn't venture this far south.

Professional *beisbol* in the Dominican Republic is played in such a way that a travelling circus with two freak shows wouldn't stand a chance against it. Believe me, they use the three strikes and four balls rule and they scratch themselves and spit a lot, but after that, *beisbol* in the DR is really quite bizarre.

For a baseball fan, watching the game played in the Dominican Republic falls somewhere between a bad dream and a good nightmare.

Many Dominicans carry guns and machetes and the vendors sell large bottles of rum at the games. This is a combination that would have forced Kelly Gruber to wear a bulletproof vest during his days as a Toronto Blue Jay.

So before you can buy a bottle of rum at a baseball game in the DR, you must first go to a room and check your weapon. You're given a ticket stub to pick it up later. This makes umpires and guys in hitting slumps feel a whole lot better.

Street urchins rule the halls of the DR stadiums. After escorting you to your seat, they clean it off with the same rags they used to clean the windows of your car in the parking lot. Though neither service is asked for, money is demanded for both.

Scalpers in the DR work *inside* the stadium. They buy blocks of tickets and then sell them to spectators who have paid the general admission price but want preferred seating.

At this particular game in San Pedro, I arrived early and went to a seat behind the home team's dugout, ignoring, as best I could, the scalper of that section. As I sat down, the bottom section of the seat next to me fell to the concrete floor.

Although the baseball fields in the Dominican Republic are things of beauty — lush green natural grass carpets laid around rich red loam infields — the seats are made of cheap plastic and have not been replaced for decades.

As the seat clattered to the floor, I looked at the scalper, he looked at me, I pointed to the fallen seat, and he picked it up and put it carefully back on its broken mountings.

During the course of batting practice, the seat fell to the ground several times, and the scalper put it back each time.

The scalper's section began filling up as game time neared, and I moved over to the next section to talk to a scout for the L.A. Dodgers before heading up to the press box. But I never took my eyes off the scalper and the seat that wouldn't stay put.

Eventually he sold every other seat in this section and was very close to a deal on the broken one, when it once more fell to the floor. After that he picked the bloody thing up and threw it over the wall at the back of the section, where it landed in a heap of garbage ten feet below. I laughed like hell, and as the scalper looked around, we made eye contact. I gave him an enthusiastic thumbs up. I'd have tossed it after the first fall.

I thought he'd leave but he stayed, and I'll be damned if he didn't sell the seatless space, at a reduced rate, for standing room only. A Dominican, not too tall and not too sober, came in late and bought the spot to watch the game with his bum against the back of the seat. I couldn't believe it. The Dodger scout was trying to tell me about the legendary size of Julian Yan's feet and I was still marvelling at what had to be the world's greatest seat scalper.

In the bottom of the fourth inning, a San Pedro batter hit a low foul ball that cleared the home team's dugout and the scalper's section behind it. Several fans jumped to catch it, but it was a little too high, carrying over the wall and into the garbage heap beyond. A couple of kids started out of their seats, but of course the short, glassy-eyed Dominican had a strategically better start — he had no seat to contend with.

Over the wall he jumped, straight into the pile of cans and bottles and rotting clippings and...and when he somehow scrambled back over the wall, that entire section of the stadium was looking at the happiest man in the Dominican Republic. Not only did he have, in his right hand, a nearly new official game baseball, but in his left hand he was waving his long-lost seat.

In a world that gets a shade weirder every day, you have to ask, how lucky can one guy get?

The Dominican returned to his standing-room-only spot, put the seat in place, sat down, and fell flat on his ass. This again brought the crowd to its feet, cheering wildly.

And, in all probability, there is your answer to the question of a man's fortune.

Long-time dictator Generalissimo Rafael Trujillo built four national baseball stadiums in such a way that he could watch the ball game from each of his palatial presidential boxes up and behind home plate but the fans could not see through the glass and catch him making love to one of his mistresses. (One-way glass is something even the SkyDome Hotel in Toronto didn't think of, though they probably wish they had on that clear night of Tuesday, May 15, 1990. Who was that unclothed couple anyway? And if she conceived, do you think they named the baby Jay?)

And for the record, watching baseball and making love simultaneously made General Trujillo a two-sport wonder long before Bo Jackson had been born.

In the DR, fanatics — fans who eat, drink, and sleep *beisbol* — occasionally dash out and run the bases carrying their club's flag. The umpire calls time, the fan slides into home plate, crosses himself, the crowd roars, and the game resumes.

For some reason, a lot of batboys on the Dominican teams are middle-aged dwarfs, but I don't think it's a league rule.

Photographers wander onto the playing field and sometimes collide with a player trying to catch a foul ball. When a fight breaks out in the stands, the game stops and the players become spectators until a decision is rendered.

Now, four months later, I can still see the duck dodging bottles and gloves, bats and balls. The fact that nobody, not even a player from either team, was able to nail the bird tells me they need Dave Winfield as much in the Dominican Republic as the Blue Jays do at the Dome when those seagulls come calling.

Still curious by game's end, I asked the sports reporter what *Linea Exclusiva De Embutidos* meant, the product on the sign the duck crashed into.

With a sick little grin of irony, he replied, "Snackmeat."

"Spam?" I asked.

"*Si,*" he said, "sim-u-lar."

As a traditional ball fan with a natural hate for mascots, I sat back and treated myself to a delicious little daydream substituting B.J. Birdy for the duck. Set to music of course . . . *one, two, three merengue!*

And dance I did on New Year's Eve.

I would have told you the story of how I welcomed in 1993 a lot sooner, but it wasn't until yesterday that I finally managed to put out the fire in my undershorts.

At precisely midnight on the last day of 1992, I was standing in front of a turquoise shack they called a bar on the main road that runs from Santo Domingo to San Pedro in the Dominican Republic

(Motto: "If It's Broke, Don't Fix It").

For you history buffs, Santo Domingo, the capital of the DR, was founded in 1501 by Christopher Columbus's little brother Bart. Honest, you could even look it up. And for you sports fans, San Pedro de Macoris is the home town of baseball star and former soccer-style outfielder for the Toronto Blue Jays, George Bell.

I wouldn't say San Pedro is a stench masquerading as a city, but the running joke in the Dominican is that although President Joaquin Balaquer is totally blind, he always knows when he's in San Pedro.

So, as the clock ticked off another year of my life, I stood on a dark stretch of bad road somewhere between Christopher Columbus's ne'er-do-well brother and a guy who in 1987 invited me, as a Toronto Blue Jay fan, to "kiss my purple butt!"

I'd never mess with anybody named Bart, and I didn't take George up on his offer — that's just the kind of guy I am.

The party at my hotel across the road had ended prematurely when the manager took to the stage and, after much pleading by the guests, agreed to do his famous once-a-year rendition of Frank Sinatra's famous hit "My Way." Unfortunately, the hotel band got a little confused and launched into Elton John's famous hit "Benny and the Jets." This actually happened and if you go to the DR, you'll see the band as soon as you arrive — they're now baggage handlers at Santo Domingo International.

By midnight I had left the party and wandered out to the highway where I stood at the side of the Avenue of the Americas with other patrons of the bar, looking over the tops of the small hotels on Juan Dolio's tourist strip and into the sky above the beach where the traditional Dominican New Year's fireworks display was definitely not exploding in majesty and splendour as advertised.

A quick downpour had dampened the fireworks, and although nothing was visible in the sky, you could hear the weak snap, crackle, and pop of gunpowder being ignited at ground level. Some local party-goers who had paid $25 each to hear the grand fireworks display began threatening to do the manager *their way.*

All of a sudden this bright orange missile shot up from the hotel directly across from us and we all had a really good look at it because it was headed directly for us. I thought it must be either the largest Roman candle in the world, or some disgruntled former hotel employee had got his hands on a Patriot Missile.

It loomed larger and louder and, although nobody would disagree that this particular bar could use a good ground-to-air missile, I think everybody would have preferred to read about it in the morning paper.

I asked the American guy behind me if he'd ever seen anything like this and he said yes, once, during the '68 Tet Offensive.

As this fireball raced down on us, it fluttered for a second, drifted slightly off course and, to everyone's amazement, the shop beside the bar, called the Foto Expresso, took a direct hit on the roof.

The Foto Expresso, I'm told, produces same-day colour prints, but it sounds like it was once in the really strong coffee business.

A shower of sparks enveloped the shop, and everybody applauded. It was the applause of joy and relief. It's not often that, while celebrating the new year, you come under friendly fire. And survive!

The plan was to shoot the fireworks off shore, and I can just imagine the manager chewing out the employee: "Rafael! I said aim for the reef not the roof, you coconut!"

I'm not sure if the Foto Expresso caught fire or not because, by then, it was midnight and time for the traditional Dominican dance — *one, two, three merengue!* Happy New Year and pass the ammunition!

And one more thing. You must be careful in the Dominican Republic because some Spanish words sound like English words but have very different meanings.

For instance, on New Year's Eve I always treat myself to one very good cigar. Normally, my once-a-year cigar is hand-rolled in Havana but tonight I'm in the DR and as I always say, when in the DR wear your medical alert bracelet at all times.

At the hotel bar I ordered my expensive *perro* and then politely asked the bartender to light it for me. At first he protested and gave me a couple of really weird looks, but in the end he did as I asked. Even in the DR, the customer is always right, even if he is suffering from battle fatique.

It turns out the Spanish word for cigar is *puro*. *Perro* means "dog."

The last time anybody saw Sparky, he was crossing the Sierra Limones Mountains in the north and still making good time.

Okay, okay, I made that up about the *puro* and the *perro*, but that stuff about the fireworks is absolutely true.

And that's it. I've had it.

I will never again attend a traditional New Year's Eve celebration in the Dominican Republic without first having direct radio access to U.S. air support.

I love this place. Why? *No se.*

Mexico – Sink the *Bora Bora!*

Imust say I had some real reservations about free trade with Mexico.

They date right from that first summit meeting between our two countries, when a high, unnamed administrative aide to Brian Mulroney burst into a top-level meeting between our prime minister and Mexican President Carlos Salinas Gortari in Mexico City with a message from home. Brian was taken aback. He figured either this aide must be high or the message was real important.

The message was important. It was the news he had dreaded for months. Outrage consumed him — his face reddened, his cute little blue blazer surged, and his jaw jutted out opening a gash over President Gortari's right eye that later took eight stitches to close. The message: "Seasonally adjusted figures released by the Department of Employment and Immigration this morning confirm that despite free trade with the United States — *some people still have jobs in Canada!*"

In order to reduce our average hourly wage rate in Canada to compete with that of the United States, Mulroney had left word before he left for Mexico that all full-time jobs in this country were to be officially eliminated. Those wanting to work temporarily would be picked up each morning at the town square and trucked out to job sites by their employers and paid a daily wage commensurate with how badly they wanted a ride home.

Ever the optimist, always the one to seize a bad moment and turn it into a catastrophe, Mulroney forced a smile and looked across the table at President Gortari, who was holding a hankie to his head.

"May I call you Gort?" Mulroney eased in.

"Sure, Ruin," replied the president.

The aide rushed out with a release for the press that our prime minister and the president of Mexico had developed a deeply personal and highly constructive relationship at their very first meeting.

"What's the average wage here in Mexico, Gort?"

"Twelve dollars, Ruin."

"Ouch! Twelve bucks an hour is pretty steep, Gort."

"That's twelve dollars a day, Ruin, and the days are very long."

"What's your largest export to Canada?"

"Sombreros."

"Not the kind with those little fluff-balls hanging from the brim!"

"Correcto."

"Wow!" exclaimed the prime minister. The barriers to trade were falling faster than the Canadian dollar after an upbeat economic forecast by Finance Minister Michael Wilson.

Brian, the consummate deal-cutter, was rolling up his sleeves. "Did you ever think of putting refried beans in cans and swapping them even-steven, for say, word processors which we make in Canada?"

"Not until now, you sweet-talking son-of-a . . . "

Brian Mulroney was out the door and onto the balcony where, to the hordes of cheering and flag-waving Mexicans, with President Gortari at his side, he announced: "The stage is set for a new era in Mexican-Canadian relations and a fresh partnership between our two countries." The thousands of Mexicans in the central plaza were stunned. First, they thought Dan Quayle was actually much taller than he looked up there on that balcony. Secondly, they couldn't get over how much their own president looked like Mikhail Gorbachev with that red stain on his forehead. They went wild. They cheered, they danced, and they sang: "Pass the tequila, Mila . . . your husband's like a Santa Claus to us."

Afraid that others might misinterpret his extravagant generosity, Prime Minister Mulroney flew immediately to the Barbados where he forgave $182 million in loan repayment that a bunch of Caribbean countries owed us. They went wild. They cheered, they danced and they sang: "Pass the bottle of rum, chum . . . we got a live one here who thinks he's Santa Claus."

No, I've always had misgivings about free trade with the States and Mexico.

In fairness though, free trade with the United States did help the unemployed, in that Simon Reisman got a real good job out of it.

But I couldn't imagine some kind of giant leap forward between one country that manufactures state-of-the-art buses and another that breeds stubborn burros, both in their own right considered mainstays of transportation.

How would this work? We would send them our Canada Space Arms, and in return they would send us wicker donkeys, the ones wearing sunglasses with the ears sticking up through the sombrero? We would ship them nuclear CANDU reactors and they would send back truckloads of black velvet paintings of bullfights in progress? We'll export cellular car phones to Mexico, and Mexico will send back the equivalent tonnage of shiny turquoise jewellery and straw shopping bags? We send them BellTel, they give us Taco Bell?

To many of us, this didn't sound like such a hot idea. Not until Brian sweetened the pot. He finished off his address in Mexico City by announcing that Mexico will not ship their goods in plastic containers or wooden crates. No sir. Instead, we'll get all their stuff wrapped in *piñatas*.

That's right, when the shipments come in, Brian's going to let us all go down to the town square and with sticks supplied by the people who missed the morning pick-up truck, we'll be able to beat the hell out of these *piñatas,* and the fruits of free trade will rain down upon our heads.

There's only one thing that worries me about the deal. If the United States got our fresh water in that free trade agreement, do we get Mexico's water in this one?

Maybe that's part of Brian's hidden agenda. With drinking water from Mexico, we'll all be way too occupied to protest.

You've got to love the guy. Coming up with free trade with Mexico so soon after the success of free trade with the United States. Like sending *The QEII* out to try and duplicate the inaugural success of *The Titanic*.

For these very reasons and at great personal expense, I travelled to Mexico over the Christmas holidays last year to assess Canada's chances of first winning and then maintaining the runner-up position in the North American Free Trade Agreement.

You see, we can't possibly win. The best we can shoot for is coming second in this tournament of three.

The United States made the rules, will implement the rules, and will rule on any disputes of the rules. As I may have mentioned, Brian did the deal, eh?

"Round and round the mulberry bush . . . " Think of NAFTA as a box of real bad surprises, and just when you're sure things could not get any worse — *pop! goes the weasel.*

(And let's just overlook the fact that the weasel is now shilling for the Montreal law firm of Ogilvy, Renault.)

So I was there, in Puerto Vallarta at 12:01 a.m., January 1, 1994, to make sure the Mexicans didn't have their fingers crossed behind their backs at the moment the deal officially kicked in.

To welcome in the new year, our hotel set off fireworks. Farther south, in Chiapis, they rounded up local government and military officials and shot them. And isn't it this kind of quaint cultural customs we're afraid of losing in NAFTA?

During the time I spent in Mexico, I drew up a short list of specific areas where I believe Canada's free trade war with Mexico will be won or lost.

The Canadian exports to Mexico mentioned in this list go beyond the obvious products like birth-control devices, Kaopectate, crowbars to open patio doors, steel-plated business suits for NAFTA negotiators, and photo I.D. buttons for the approximately 75 million men in Mexico named Rafael.

Asbestos underwear: I'm sure you've probably seen a fireworks display called a burning house in which the first floor of the wicker structure goes off with a spark-spewing bang. This ignites the second floor which goes off with even more sparks and louder bangs and so on until all four tiers explode en mass with rockets shooting into the sky to erupt and fall to earth in brightly flared embers.

You've seen one of those, right? But have you ever seen a man *in* the house during the fire?

Honest, at our hotel a fat guy wearing ordinary civilian clothes, and showing a bit of butt cleavage to boot, stood on stage at 12:01 a.m. New Year's Day, inside the burning house as it exploded, caught fire, and burned to the ground around him.

His name was Pedro. In Canada, he'd be called Four-Alarmer.

I've seen elaborate and even dangerous fireworks displays before, but I've never actually seen somebody wear them.

In order that Pedro can pass on this tradition to his sons, I think asbestos underwear would make an ideal Canadian export to Mexico. That and a fire-retardant underarm deodorant.

Friendliness: Forget it. We could never compete with Mexicans in the areas of attitude and hospitality as shown to me by my Aeromexico pilot who invited me into the cockpit of his DC-10 to enlighten me how he and his two co-pilots — at the centre of a state-of-the-art computer terminal with a hundred flashing lights and several hundred fail-safe switches — do tequila shooters. (Not really, but the navigator and I voted for it.)

Alarm clocks: I'm not a stickler for punctuality, especially while on vacation, but our Sunset Tour of the Puerto Vallarta coast left ten minutes late.

Normally this would be fine, but the pre-recorded cassette pointing out the highlights along the coast started on time. Subsequently, this meant city hall was located, according to the guide tape, at Carlos O'Brien's Bar and Grill, Christopher Columbus was a guy selling pistachios on the main street, and the lagoon where Richard Burton proposed to Elizabeth Taylor during the filming of *The Night of the Iguana* was a Domino's Pizza outlet.

Annoyance-seeking homing devices: For Canadian tourists who visit Mexico over the holidays, I think a big seller would be a shoulder-launched rocket carrying a small payload which would seek out and destroy any sound system playing the song *Feliz Navidad*.

Meatometers: A combination thermometer and identifier, this little device, when stuck into a piece of meat, would tell you how hot it is and what kind of meat it is. For Canadian tourists, this would be a big help. There seem to be a great many afternoon hot dogs in Mexico impersonating sausage at the next morning's breakfast.

The food was very good and plentiful. I just got a little nervous when the two stray dogs I made friends with at the Manager's Welcome to Mexico Party failed to show up at the Adios Barbecue.

But the real dangers for Canadians travelling to Mexico is not the music, the food, or the water. No, the real danger for Canadians in Mexico may be finding themselves in a perilous predicament at the hands of desperate people like John and Marrita Pearce of Fort Erie, Ontario.

John and Marrita are very nice people, but a little on the strange side, which is what attracted me to them in the first place.

It started out innocently enough with a shared taxi into the town of Puerto Vallarta from our hotel 30 kilometres to the north. After that, it was a drink, some stories swapped under grass huts on the beach, and then they sprang the trap: "How about going on the *Bora Bora* cruise?"

The *Bora Bora* cruise is advertised as an exciting day of sailing, snorkelling, swimming, walking or horseback riding to a jungle waterfall, lunch, and an all-day open bar.

For $43 U.S. per person, it's my ideal vacation day and, if the others feel they must sail, snorkel, swim, walk, and horseback in that kind of heat, I wish them all the best.

We arrived at the pier in Puerto Vallarta as a party of four — roughly twice the size of the federal Progressive Conservative Party — John, Marrita, me, and a woman who has recently and miraculously begun speaking to me again.

We became a little concerned when the captain of the trimaran *Bora Bora* told us this sailboat, with twenty plastic lawn chairs taking up all the room on the deck, actually had a capacity of ninety passengers. He then proceeded to board the 150 people waiting in line ahead of us.

Marrita led the mutiny based on safety, comfort, and John's quick mathematical calculation that by eleven a.m. the boat would be out of beer.

Before we could hail a cab to return to the hotel, somebody semi official looking interceded and, in minutes, we were following the *Bora Bora* out of port aboard the luxurious *Vallarta Sol*.

We had the entire top deck to ourselves, an abundance of high-quality plastic lawn chairs, and Chillo. Chillo, our on-board, personal-performance waiter, was on a mission to deliver the most

Corona splits to the least number of tourists on a one-day cruise in the history of Mexican tourism.

John's job was to make sure Chillo was not denied his dream. My job was to back up John and, above all, keep him from becoming bait for trolling.

As a group, we danced and taunted the 150 passengers on our nearby sister ship, the *Bora Bora*, who by this time had congealed in the hot sun.

Adventure # 1: Snorkelling *Los Arches*.

Los Arches are lava deposits that rise majestically above the swells in beautiful Banderas Bay, and I cannot describe the experience — no, the sheer thrill — of diving below that sea-green surface to examine the sub-oceanic underbelly of, you guessed it, 150 snorkellers from the *Bora Bora*.

The most interesting were those sixty above-capacity passengers snorkelling without snorkels. A kid selling oxygen at *Los Arches* could have put himself through college that day.

I had a rather nasty collision with one of the *arches* and returned to ship. Chillo, who doubles as the *Vallarta Sol's* paramedic (and in this capacity has the authority to marry injured people at sea), doubled my dosage of Corona.

Adventure # 2: The Quimixto jungle hike.

Normally trudging two miles uphill through dense jungle wearing shorts and tennis shoes is not high on my list of things to do on my holidays. But this was a real challenge because the trail for hikers up to the waterfall is the same trail used for horseback riders.

Normally, in Mexican jungles, you would try to avoid poisonous snakes and guerrillas who are really ticked off about NAFTA, but on this trail, the trick was to not step on — you guessed it — the steamers of 150 horses ridden by passengers of the *Bora Bora*, who arrived an hour before us.

The Quimixto jungle survival rule? When you stop stepping on horse buns, you're lost. Double back to the main trail.

The Mexican sun was a searing, relentless ball of . . . oh, sorry, that was the glow coming off of John.

Adventure # 3: Successfully shooting the Quimixto Falls.

The Quimixto Falls is a roaring, rushing cascade of cold mountain water so secluded, so beautiful that explorer Hernando Cortez, in 1519, could not help but open a patio lounge and tequila-popper bar just a few feet from the brink.

The water is so cold and so fast that nobody swims under the falls except those who want to die at this point of the tour.

I swam. The challenge here was to actually negotiate the slow-moving line up at the falls bar which was being held hostage by approximately sixty ex-*Bora Bora* passengers refusing to return to the ship.

Jungle residents for miles around stopped their machetes and spears in mid-swing as the chant went up: *"Sink the Bora Bora! Sink the Bora Bora!"*

Adventure # 4: Keeping John from carrying out his promise to marry Chillo and spend the rest of his life as a purser on the *S.S. Vallarta Sol.*

Adventure # 5: Talking the women into re-creating the details of the *Bora Bora* cruise the next morning, so I could write this report.

I love Mexico. I really do. And I'll be back just as soon as they let me.

Edmonton – Thick Steaks
and Thin Skins

As I mentioned in the introduction, my main motive in writing this book was to draw attention to the recent loss of laughter among a people noted for their wonderful sense of humour. Edmonton — a great place for steaks but a bit thin in the skin — is where I witnessed our national mirth being put on a stretcher and taken to the morgue on a dark day in February 1992.

Here then is the column that turned out to be the first salvo in the shoot-out at the Not-So-OK Corral.

Last month I travelled to Edmonton, Alberta, and got a close-up look at the Wild, Wild West.

Edmonton is an isolated, northern settlement of tall commercial buildings surrounded by squat, sprawling residential buildings inhabited by 800,000 people who ought to be airlifted out by military helicopters for their own good.

The Falkland Islands are more in touch with the real world than Edmonton, Alberta, and the islanders don't get involved in sex between their consenting farm animals. While I was in Edmonton — why should I make this up? — their Swine Artificial Insemination Centre was up for sale.

Alberta Agriculture gave no reason why it felt the need to artificially conduct the reproduction process of pigs in a science laboratory — a process, I might add, that seems to be progressing quite well naturally, every time I visit a farm here in Wainfleet.

In Edmonton, hogs are definitely not "as happy as a pig in . . . " They're just not allowed to be.

No asking price was listed for the swine semen centre, and as far as I could determine, Peter Pocklington was not involved.

While I was in Edmonton, Steven West was on the front page of local newspapers for one week straight.

Steve West, a veterinarian by profession, was the newly named solicitor general of Alberta and as such had provincial policing, liquor law enforcement, impaired driving, and family violence among his responsibilities.

Soon after his appointment, his first wife came forth with allegations that he beat her up, and, after their divorce, his wages had to be garnisheed to secure court-ordered support payments.

A fellow veterinarian accused West of beating two dogs.

West admitted to spending nights in jail for drinking offences and to being part of a vigilante group trying to rid his home town of drug dealers.

Others claimed that Steve West had been a belligerent drunk, insulting customers in bars, and that he once trashed a kid's mountain bike in his neighbour's backyard.

And in light of all these allegations — and this is the best part — Solicitor General Steve West vehemently denied having beaten up the dogs!

West offered to abstain from drinking alcohol as long as he was the solicitor general of Alberta.

And believe it or not, his fellow cabinet colleagues and Tory legislature members, along with Premier Don Getty, backed him 100 percent. Sure. With Steve on the wagon, it means just that much more for them.

They celebrate marriage a little differently out west. At least they did in nearby Red Deer where, when I was there, they were just getting around to sorting out who in the wedding party would go to jail and for how long.

Three separate fights were in progress at the house reception by the time the Mounties arrived, and those who weren't arrested, were hospitalized. One man was stabbed with a butter knife, one man was whacked with a pool cue, and yet another man had his ring finger bitten off. Two bits of good news here. The wedding ring was not on the finger that was bitten off and, more important, the solicitor general of Alberta was not in attendance.

While I was there, Mickey Mouse was suing the West Edmonton Mall over the rights to the word *Fantasyland,* and by the time I left, this somehow didn't seem so unusual.

I visited the West Edmonton Mall, the world's largest retail theme park, and they have more submarines than the Canadian Navy. The submarines that take children on underwater rides are, of course, different than our military ships. The ones at the mall work.

The next time we go to war against Saddam Hussein, I think we could exact a quick and decisive victory if we can somehow lure the Iraqis to the West Edmonton Mall, then ambush them by submarine somewhere near the main food court.

I attended a party in Edmonton where forty screaming, inebriated people with way too much time on their hands (curlers) went absolutely loony over — get this — the limbo.

I am not making this up. A decade after the limbo died a well-deserved death on its island of origin, people in Edmonton get delirious as they lurch and jerk pelvis-first under a horizontal curling broom.

This is scary. I definitely do not want to be anywhere near Edmonton when those people find out about individually wrapped cheese slices. Can you imagine the celebration?

But seriously, it's not Edmonton's fault. This is an isolated and deprived city. I mean, it's nearly a three-hour drive to the nearest big American city — Calgary.

And that's the news from the Wild, Wild West, where men are men and women would like to see that changed through modern surgical techniques.

Well, the ink was barely dry on that column when the Edmonton *Sun* responded with two shots to my back. A disgruntled ex-Edmontonian in Hamilton contacted the *Sun* and the editorial staff rose courageously to defend an indignant citizenship that was not yet aware of the indignity and hence not in need of defence.

Not one but two reporters from the Edmonton *Sun* were assigned to have at me. You have to understand that in Canada, the *Sun* is widely considered to be as trashy as a newspaper can get without running Elvis headlines in every other edition.

Reporter Tom Philip, smelling a Pulitzer Prize opportunity, raced down to the Edmonton Chamber of Commerce and asked president Fred Windwick if he thought that Edmonton was "an isolated northern settlement" whose inhabitants "ought to be air-lifted out by military helicopters for their own good."

And I know you're going to find this hard to believe, but the president of the Chamber went on record as saying "no."

"It's not true, it's not factual and frankly, it's a little insulting," claimed the president. Well, the skeletal facts in the column were true and remained so even after I liberally editorialized around them. As far as "insulting" goes, I have never beat a wife, a dog or a bicycle, nor have I ever bitten off anyone's ring finger. I kicked a car once but it started it.

Reporter Kerry Diotte, in yet another edition of the paper, wrote a column in which he reprinted the most inciting observations from my column about the city and its people, omitting all of the five factual points of the article save for the Swine Artificial Insemination Centre.

He began his column by calling me "a mealy-mouthed columnist from southern Ontario." I couldn't believe it. Either this guy took a wild but lucky stab in the dark or he'd spoken to my mother first.

He finished his column by referring to my home town of Port Colborne, Ontario, and calling it "a slagheap situated on that stinkpond known as Lake Erie." Again I was shocked. When it comes to slagheaps situated on Lake Erie, I and every man, woman, and child of the town of Port Colborne would defend to death the right of Buffalo, New York, to exist.

This reporter also printed the telephone and fax numbers of the Hamilton *Spectator*, one of thirty newspapers that carry my column, and urged Edmontonians to wreak revenge.

After I hung up on reporter Diotte for being rude, accusatory, and asking me how much money I earned, he gave my number to some rube who called and, refusing to identify himself, accused me of being, among other things, a donor to the Swine Artificial Insemination Centre.

I vehemently denied this, and just because my eighty-seven-year-old mother, who happened to be listening in on the extension, laughed so hard she had to be sedated, it didn't mean it was true.

Edmontonians went a bit ballistic. A full page of irate letters to the editor of the Hamilton *Spectator* was published, and those were only the ones fit for a family newspaper. Several subscribers to the *Spectator* cancelled delivery of the paper. Radio talk shows in both Edmonton and Calgary used the column for lively anti-East open-line shows.

A reporter for the Calgary *Sun* did a column off of Kerry Diotte's column on my column.

As previously mentioned, I was named "Asshole of the Month" in Edmonton which, at the very least, gave Peter Pocklington a bit of break.

Another guy sent me a letter indicating he was coming east that summer and would drop by to take care of me and the problem. I've since had his threatening letter examined by the Centre for Forensic Science in Toronto, but even the most modern handwriting analysis scanners cannot pick up on Crayola.

I may have accused Edmontonians of strange behaviour, but I could never point a finger at them for beating around the bush. One note began: "First of all, you're full of shit." It ended sarcastically with "Hamilton is the honeywagon of the Canadian East."

In the midst of all the calls for my head and other seemingly unrelated parts from Edmonton *Sun* readers, the column in the Calgary *Sun* claimed Calgarians loved my take on Edmonton. Apparently, a Calgary alderman by the name of Richard Magnus was in Edmonton when the controversy erupted and the whole thing had him in stitches. He apparently believed every bad thing I had to say about Edmonton was true and passed around copies back home to prove it. Don't you just love cross-province rivalries?

The Edmonton *Sun* failed to demonstrate the same impassioned enthusiasm for freedom of speech as they had shown for manipulating the emotions of their readers in order to sell more papers. When the Alberta Press Council, on my behalf, asked Patrick Harden, the publisher of the *Sun*, to print a letter to the editor explaining to Edmontonians my side of the controversy, his reply by letter, was:

It's unfortunate that you have to waste the Alberta Press Council's time and money in responding to complaints such as that from Mr. William Thomas of Port Colborne, Ontario.

You should simply have ignored it — as we will.

Sincerely,

Patrick Harden

So you see the Edmonton *Sun* can and does laugh — when it comes to fair comment and free speech.

To date, the *Sun* has refused to join the Alberta Press Council. It's my belief they will continue to do so as long as the Alberta Press Council maintains journalistic standards.

Oh yeah, I said I wouldn't apologize but I will, publicly, right here, to reporter Kerry Diotte.

Kerry, I'm sorry. After I read that you had called me "mealy-mouthed" and said I lived in "a slagheap . . . on a stinkpond," I got so darn angry, I took a pencil and drew dark, little curls on the photo of you at the top of your column. On top, Kerry, where your hair used to be. I'm sorry I did that.

III

Ten Things I Can't Seem to Get My Head Around

Root Canal – The Pain
Is in the Payment

I got mugged the other day by a guy wearing a mask, and I was sitting in a dentist's chair at the time. I hate when that happens.

Does anybody remember a time long ago when your biggest fear in going to the dentist was *his* drill and not *your* personal bankruptcy?

In the last couple years, I needed root canal work done on two teeth. This involves going to my regular dentist who spots the problem then refers me to the Big "E," the King of Cavities, the Duke of Dentistry — the Endodontist.

If you look carefully at an endodontist's business card, you'll see the middle initial is always "$". It's a secret code.

Now I have nothing against my regular dentist. He always explains the procedures, then asks me periodic questions while he's working on me, knowing my answer is always "Gughunnonagahngheen."

Besides being friendly and a good tennis player, my regular dentist only wants to be a millionaire.

My endodontist wants to go to a Jays game knowing he nets more a year than the cleanup hitter. He dreams of knocking Bill Gates off the cover of *Forbes Magazine*. He aspires to steal *The Marla* away from *The Donald*.

For root canal therapy on two teeth, the endodontist charged me $1,412.

Not counting the time he spent with other patients while I lay horizontal, listening to the sound of my own saliva being sucked out of my body with more tools in my mouth than I can carry in the trunk of my car, it took him a total of two hours' work.

Now $700 an hour is definitely a major league wage. It may even sound excessive. But if you compare an endodontist's wage, using the time unit of an "hour," hold on the $700 figure, and use the time unit of a "week" for the rest of us, then it's not all that bad.

But in fairness, this figure also includes a fifteen-minute consultation in which a dental technician takes X-rays and the endodontist issues his expert opinion. For the second session, I called to book an appointment to have the work done, but they insisted I come down for a consultation session even though they had already taken the X-rays and made the diagnosis.

And I have to admit, experts are seldom wrong. If I had not been there, in person, I never would have been able to witness the endodontist holding those X-rays up to the light and saying: "Uh huh, uh huh, uh huh, okay. Book an appointment with the receptionist."

I don't mean to underscore the value of the consultation session. It's a crucial life-determining test in which the receptionist decides whether your heart can stand the estimate.

Endodontist receptionists are hired for their unique ability to giggle internally while delivering the details with a straight face.

"The therapy is going to cost $716 for four canals," she said. "How will you be paying?"

How about letting me take out a second mortgage on the first root canal which I now own outright?

Didn't dentists used to bill patients? At the endodontist's, it's Visa, MasterCard, or cheque.

Perhaps it's because he had me laid low and flat on my back, but my endodontist felt he had to talk down to me.

"What exactly is root canal therapy?" I asked.

Believing I'd used up all my brain power on the morning comics, his measured reply was: "Ah, let's just say your tooth died."

I'm not surprised, I thought. It was probably my eye tooth — it saw the bill coming before I did!

Anyway, I now own two teeth brought back from the dead which, when you include canals, caps, and crowns, cost $2,612 or approximately twice as much as I paid for my first two cars.

And wouldn't you know it, they're way in the back where I can't show them off. Which is why I paid an extra $24.95 and had a tiny rear-view mirror mounted on my nose.

It's strange, but with all that money tied up in my molars, I now feel I should eat only in really expensive restaurants.

Do you see what's happening here? We're so busy making fun of rich doctors injuring themselves by tripping over their investment portfolios and so busy comparing greedy lawyers to highway roadkill, we didn't notice when the dentists slipped in the side door and stole the family jewels.

This dawned on us only when they melted them down and sold them back to us as caps and crowns and bridges.

Have you noticed today's dentists wear masks? Not only is it an effective hygienic precaution, but it also makes identifying them in a police line-up a lot more difficult.

"Say, stranger, who was that masked man anyway?"

"Gughunnorahahngheen."

They don't have those little rinsing bowls beside the dental chair anymore. It's just a hunch, but I think a lot of patients, when told to rinse and spit, were missing the bowl on purpose.

For the endodontist it was either get rid of the bowl or start wearing galoshes during work hours.

And at the end, they always ask: "Do you have a dental plan?"

I do now. In fact I have two plans.

The next time my dental X-rays come back showing any kind of problem, I'm going to take them to Niagara Photo and have them retouched.

And from now on, dead teeth get a proper burial under my pillow. In keeping with the industry, surely the tooth fairy must now be trading in mutual funds instead of nickels and dimes.

The Girl Guides
Versus the Jehovahs

Canada? Yet another tinderbox in this vile and volatile world? We just don't know how close we came last year to an all-out civil war in this country.

In mid-March of '94 the Girl Guides of Canada announced they were dropping the Queen from their membership oath, and in retaliation the Monarchist League of Canada threatened to boycott Girl Guide cookies. Honest. This actually happened.

And as if this were not enough civil unrest for one week, the Jehovah's Witnesses began refusing to acknowledge the Canadian national anthem, and staunch nationalists were seeing flag-red. This also is true.

This kind of cross-country sniping and community chaos just naturally had to stop. And fortunately it did before we were all bathed in blood. It stopped before we started reading news reports like:

• Today, in retaliation for the monarchists' boycott of their cookies, the Girl Guides of Canada announced that they will refuse street-crossing assistance to any little old lady wearing a Union Jack pin.

• Noticing a lot of people standing around on curbs, ultra-nationalists began sneaking up behind them with boom boxes and playing the national anthem.

• Furious at being left stranded on curbs across Canada, little-old-lady monarchists vowed to put Union Jack pins in apples when Girl Guides come calling next Halloween.

• Upset that the Guides also made the reference to God optional in their pledge, Jehovah's Witnesses today filed a lawsuit against the Girl Guides of Canada over door-to-door territorial rights.

• Public protests took place in all major Canadian cities yesterday as thousands of uniformed young girls stood at attention in front of Jehovah's Witness Halls and hummed the national anthem.

• Furious over yesterday's anthem protests, Jehovah's Witnesses announced today that residences where Girl Guides live will now have to pay for each issue of *The Watchtower*. They may take out a subscription, but they won't get the luggage or alarm-clock bonus.

• In a move that their national organization does not condone, Girl Guides began scraping the cream filling out of all cookies ordered by known Jehovah's Witnesses.

• In what first appeared to be a conciliatory move, the Jehovah's Witnesses have stated they will now play the national anthem at meetings. Further questioning revealed, however, that they're going to use the Robert Goulet version.

• After one entire week of standing on curbs with the national anthem blaring in their ears, little-old-lady monarchists began clubbing ultra-nationalists with their parasols. Some male monarchists, referring to this as caning, welcomed the idea.

• In a move that would in effect financially cripple the Girl Guides of Canada organization, the Jehovah's Witnesses today made an offer to Christie Foods to sell cookies door-to-door themselves. The argument of the Jehovah's Witnesses is: "Hey! We're going there anyway!"

• An ugly incident occurred on the Bloor Street subway today in Toronto when an ultra-nationalist, a monarchist, a Jehovah's Witness, and a Girl Guide all entered the same car, apparently by coincidence. Five skinheads who were beaten up and admitted to hospital claimed they were just minding their own business.

• Angered by the bad publicity they've been getting in Canada, Jehovah's Witnesses today said they are going to shun Canadian households. Starting next Sunday, when they come to your door they *are* going to take no for an answer.

As I said, we just don't know how close we came to national chaos nor how lucky we were to avoid it. We damn near had to bring our peacekeepers home from the Balkans and put them to work on *our* streets. The only other option was divine intervention. I can see it now, Canada's Second Coming — the fathers of Confederation descend upon the earth and give every Canadian a real good slap. People belonging to special-interest groups get two slaps.

The Great Carolina Turkey Shoot

We had a chance to put the cork on high-tech reproduction before the first test-tube babies were conceived. Instead, we accepted it as casually as ordering off the all-new menu of procreation — and infants under glass came up as the "special of the day."

Now a whole generation of test-tube babies are about to enter the primary school system believing the best and brightest among them could some day become Waterford Crystal.

Today children are created by means of sperm banks, egg donations, surrogate mothers, anonymous fathers, frozen embryos, and, in the case of rock star Michael Jackson, a high-priced cosmetic surgeon.

As I mentioned before, I don't understand this stuff. When I heard a woman say she'd been fertilized in-vitro, I thought Vitro must be one of those towns across the border where the bars stay open late.

I remember once seeing a cartoon of a beautiful and elegant lady entering a sperm back through the front door as a seedy, bald, badly dressed, cigar-smoking dwarf emerged through the back, counting a wad of cash. I thought it was funny, but I don't suppose a single mom who had been artificially inseminated would laugh too hard, especially years later when she gets a call from her son's teacher on his first day of school reporting: "Basil's not half as big as the rest of the kids in kindergarten."

Like most people, I have gone along with all this artificial insemination business, because frankly it has not affected me directly.

Until yesterday.

(Warning: The following story contains graphic descriptions that could make carbonated liquid come out of your nose if you're drinking ginger ale while you read it. I could not make this up even if high on laughing gas with a rubber chicken dangling from each of my ears.)

Yesterday, a reader faxed me an Associated Press news story that described how Janet Johnson of Cary, North Carolina, after failing to get pregnant by some of the higher-tech means I mentioned, had her sister Julie artificially inseminate her with a turkey baster. (Please re-read warning in previous paragraph.)

The article explained how Janet Johnson sterilized a $2.95 turkey baster in her dishwasher, and then got her husband to "make his genetic contribution" to the project. (The article does not explain if Janet Johnson laughed until she snorgled while watching husband Mark have sex with a turkey baster. It's just something I thought of in passing.)

Janet then went to her sister's house, where Julie inseminated her in an upside-down position (that's Janet who's upside down) after which she (still Janet) stood on her head for thirty minutes after each treatment.

"I figured gravity couldn't hurt," Julie said. No, certainly not. Neither would ten sessions with a reputable psychiatrist, but then that wouldn't be half as much fun.

Do you get the feeling that way too much blood is rushing to the collective heads of Janet Johnson and sister Julie?

I can't tell you how much this story has distressed me.

Since the project required numerous "treatments," I worry that the next news flash in this story will have Mark running off to Mexico to marry the turkey baster.

And you have to ask yourself if the baby, which is due later this month, is not named Tom, are not the Johnsons missing out on the comic opportunity of this century? This kid could be the poster boy for Thanksgiving for as long as he lives.

But when the kid asks Mommy where babies come from and she says K-Mart, do you get the feeling the story about the stork is actually more probable than the truth?

Yesterday, the Johnson clan of Cary, North Carolina, ruined Thanksgiving for me, forever. I don't think I could ever baste a turkey again without wondering if it was as good for the turkey as it was for me. No, I'm sorry, but it's ham at my house from here on in.

Folks, these high-tech procreation high jinks have just naturally got to stop. What's next? Sperm tablets delivered by a sling shot? Or a sperm-tipped rubber arrow and the husband dressed up as Cupid? Somebody's going to get hurt here.

I want inseminating by turkey baster outlawed in Canada before it even begins, and I hope you'll all get behind me . . . I hope you'll all support me on this one.

I know this sounds crazy, but I say let's take sex off the kitchen utensil shelf and put it back in the bedroom. Artificial insemination eliminates not only sex but the usefulness of the male reproduction equipment. In another, apparently unrelated, item in today's newspaper, the headline read: "Men Blamed for Most Faulty Genes." And I for one am not surprised — it's rust!

Public Breast Feeding
– I'm Against It

Recently, I was witness to one of life's little car accidents, and today I'm coming forth to testify on my behalf. Honest, it wasn't my fault.

It was noon hour. I was alone and minding my own business waiting for my bowl of soup to arrive in the Blue Star Restaurant in Welland, Ontario. The Blue Star is one of those old main street restaurants that serves the four-cracker pack with the soup, and when you ask for the no-smoking section, the waitress always says, no matter where you're sitting: "You're in it." Yes, it's just a very small section.

We who eat in these old booth-and-counter treasures wouldn't be caught dead in a *ristorante*. We figure if the owner can't spell the word restaurant, how good can the alphabet soup be?

As a steamy bowl of fish chowder was placed in front of me, I punched the living daylights out of my little pack of crackers — and a baby cried out in the booth in front of me.

Instinctively, I looked up at the woman holding a doll-sized infant which she effortlessly shifted from one hand to the other like a seasoned fullback would a football. Deftly, she slipped a baby blanket over her left shoulder, pulled her sweater up and mostly over her right shoulder, and . . . (for anyone who thinks I'm making this up, the waitress who was just then delivering my ice water could corroborate my story and would no doubt be here today, in this column with you and me, except that she's down at the health services office browsing through pamphlets on tubal ligation) . . . and what emerged from beneath that sweater could only be described as the mother of all mammary glands.

My first reaction was that it wasn't real. I thought, Why those clever Japanese, they've gone and invented an artificial body part that's normal and natural in every way except it's the size of Carnduff, Saskatchewan.

Referring to it as a mere breast is like calling the CN Tower an antenna.

I probably should have got up and left, but I believe I was there first.

Had there been a cup there, between me and this gland (and there most definitely was not!), its name might as well have been Dixie.

I don't mean to dwell on this, but suffice to say this particular mammary gland had the ability to reason and its own postal code.

I went into a state of temporary mental confusion commonly called shock.

The waitress left with my ice water still in her hand, and it's funny but I don't remember her hair being teased straight out like that when she came to my table.

The baby fell silent, but it may have been fright. No matter how old you are, I think you have to be a little leery about drinking from anything that's bigger than you are.

99

But he did. Oh, how he did drink. I will not go into detail except to say this was without a doubt the monster truck pull of public breast feeding.

I lost all track of time, and I suppose I just stared. It seemed like an awful long time elapsed, but then how would I know? My watch had stopped at the moment of great revelation, an event that a man more religious than myself might have taken as some sort of sign.

Such as human nature is, it was virtually impossible not to look. And yes, I'm sure many men have told that to the judge after being spotted on apartment balconies, nose flattened against the windowpane.

But right there in the fogginess of my mind a voice said: "Do you want me to warm that up for you?"

And I thought, no, please — tell me that they're not going to provide this woman with some sort of microwave device that could be adjusted to fit around . . . it was my waitress, and she was pointing at my soup.

"It was hot when I brought it," she said, walking off with a bowl of gel that used to be fish chowder.

Now I know the issue of public breast feeding has been widely debated, and I do not mean to lay bare the. . . I do not mean to again unclothe what has been . . . (I'm experiencing some severe flashbacks here so could you, just this once, finish that sentence yourself?)

Two questions still nag at me even now that I'm off the I.V. machine.

First, can this kind of baby care in restaurants be limited to just breast feeding? I for one never want to be greeted by a maître d' with: "But I'm so sorry, monsieur, the only thing I have is a table for two next to the Huggies Terminal." I'm the guy waiters most like to seat next to the kitchen door; there's no way I'm going to sit next to the diaper station. Forget it.

100

Second, and the real point I'm trying to make in recounting this story: Is this a form of discrimination? Have my civil rights in fact been violated? I mean why should the kid get his food instantly when I have to wait up to twenty minutes to get a bowl of soup?

I'm still a little woozy and like anyone who's survived a traumatic ordeal, I feel fortunate. The way I see it, if this woman had twins with coinciding hunger cycles, I'd be a dead man today.

To get a woman's opinion, when I got home I asked my eighty-seven-year-old mother how she felt about breast feeding me in public. I guess she's against it too. She quietly backed into her room and locked the door. That was last Friday. She's due out any day now.

Marriage – With No Chance of Parole

Recently, both an American and a Canadian survey on the subject of marriage produced startling statistical evidence that most women don't want to get married. The report also produced a consensus of complaints that men are slobs who just want someone to take care of them.

Hey! Hey! Hey! Wait one Wainfleet minute here! I'd be the first to admit I have, on occasion, drooled on myself, and some of my shirts have so many mustard stains they appear to be fashionably tie-dyed, but someone to take care of me? You start bad-mouthing my mom and you got a fight on your hands for sure!

According to the survey, many women characterized marriage as "legalized slavery" and "an institution of bondage." Come on now, seriously. If marriage is really an act of slavery or bondage with handcuffs, shackles, and whips, then how come Madonna is still single? Huh?

Men were only slightly more enamoured of the institution of marriage, saying things like "terrible mistake," "all the women I meet are slobs," and "my wife is a pig," which raises the question: Where, oh where, does Tom Arnold find the time to fill out all these survey questionnaires?

I myself was married once and, near the end, my wife was thoroughly convinced our marriage was made in Detroit, on the Friday afternoon of a holiday weekend.

I wouldn't say people enter into marriage with unreal expectations, but have you ever noticed the incredible similarity between the words *marriage* and *mirage*? Coincidence?

Think about it. Women wear white at the wedding, the colour of purity and goodness. Men wear black, a selection from Satan's own closet. Coincidence? I don't think so.

The ailing state of the condition of marriage is not the fault of the woman. It's the man. One man. The first married man. The man who said: "So the deal is from this day forward, I can never again date women, drink with my buddies, or howl at the moon with my ol' dog Deeter, and . . . and if it doesn't work out, you're legally entitled to half of everything I own? Okay, where do I sign?"

This is the guy who should have taken a bullet so the rest of us could be free. Find that man, exhume his body, open the brain cavity, and you'll find a place where robins used to go to nest.

Not that the first woman to get married was a candidate for a Smarties commercial either.

"So you get the career, you manage the money, your drunken brother-in-law lives on our couch while your mother tells us both how to run our lives, and as a reward I get to carry three pudgy human beings around in my stomach for twenty-seven months. Gee, when we get to Niagara Falls, can we get one of those honeymoon suites with the heart-shaped tub and the mirrors on the ceiling?" No Alberta Einstein, if you know what I mean.

Part of the problem of marriage is people marry total strangers. Remember, everybody else in your immediate family is tied to you by flesh and blood, while your husband is a lonely guy with a stupid smile who picked you up on a slow night at a bar called Koo Koo Bananas.

This is why I think brothers and sisters should be able to marry. (Please, like marriage itself, this statement was made solely for the sake of argument. Do not try this at home. In Canada, blood relatives are forbidden to marry, a law which you'll recall, when passed, caused riots in the streets of New Brunswick.)

Let's say you're a guy and you're thinking of marrying your sister. This is a person you have history with: the snake down her back, the pee in the perfume bottle, and the intimate secrets you told her first boyfriend for twenty-five cents each. You've been through a lot together, and she's always been kind enough not to press charges.

So you know this person very well. This is not a person who is likely to shake you awake at three a.m. and say, "I don't think I know you anymore." Of course she knows you. You're the one who cut the cheese during church service once and Mom slapped her for giggling. Oh, yeah, she knows you all right.

If men married their sisters, there would be no such thing as divorce. When you get to the point where you can't stand each other, you don't split up, you just go back to sleeping in your old rooms.

And if the fighting continues, there would be no need for lawyers. Mom would step in. She'd listen to both sides, offer a little homespun advice, and then haul off and whack one of you.

Think about this: Never again would you be tormented by a brother-in-law because now all the weird and annoying little creeps in the family would be your very own offspring.

Men of the Nineties
– Life After the Slice

Men of the nineties. Can you not remember the last time you had sex? Is your prostate burning like an overheated rad hose? When you walk, does it sound like others are shuffling along behind you? Oh, sorry. That's another story I'm working on entitled "Men in Their Nineties."

But seriously, the state of the straight human male of the nineties is one of dire disrepair.

In the eighties, men struggled through an era of emotional detachment from women, and now we live in fear of physical dismemberment by them.

I wouldn't say the moment Lorena sliced off John Wayne's gillooly had a profound effect on men the world over, but I can assure you that between the beginning of time and that fateful day, we never once considered keeping our reproductive organs in a wall safe at night!

Men (and many would say deservedly so) are struggling through the nineties abused, bruised, and accused by every female with a finger to wag. Our new motto is: "Okay, I did it. I'm sorry."

We used to be hunters of animals and seducers of women, and when we occasionally got the two mixed up, we coined the phrase: "Now that's entertainment!"

We went from being providers and spouses to soul mates and house husbands, and now we've been reduced to standing in the hallway looking down our pajama bottoms yelling: "Honey! Have you seen my whatchmacallit?"

We're a battered and rusting machine, running low on testosterone and badly in need of a manual. Not that we'd ever actually read one, because that's the kind of guys we are.

Frankly — and I speak for approximately seventy-five times the number of Canadian males who would actually admit to it — most men of the nineties are a bunch of middle-aged stupid straight guys who believe they were better off in the good old days when sex was something special, something private — just between you and your *National Geographic*.

I'd like to think of myself as far superior to this group of feeble-minded males who live their shallow lives bumping into walls of the maze they created, trying to understand today's women. I'd like to think of myself as way above all that, but the fact is I'm not just a member of the club, I'm their chief spokesman and official apologist.

As such, I believe the question that must be addressed here is: What does everybody want out of this anyway?

What do men want? First and foremost, some very tough legislation barring the possession of Ginsu knives in the bedroom.

After that, it's simple. Men want a woman who is attractive, a woman who matches their intellect, a woman who fulfils their basic needs. That's it. And, I might add with a certain amount of swagger, I have found my perfect woman. The only problem is, when she springs a leak, I have to put her back in the box and ship her all the way back to the Dunlop Rubber Company in Milwaukee. Can you believe it! Two hundred dollars plus tax and shipping and you don't even get one of those little patch kits!

Okay, so what do women want in a man?

In trying to make ourselves over into the men women want us to be, we have evolved from Tarzan to Tiny Tim and a lot of forgettable models in between. But that's okay — the vines were giving us a serious rash anyway.

We have gone from being he-man protectors and providers to she-like flower-sniffers and sobbing huggers. In each case as men attempted to accommodate women, they became more like them.

Now the perfect man, in the eyes of women, is a man who is sensitive, who nurtures, who boldly shows his feminine side. And now the process of forced evolution is complete: from Tarzan to Tiny Tim to . . . *Fabio!*

Fabio is the perfect man for women. He looks like Tarzan, he has the sensitivity of Tiny Tim, and as far as showing his female side, well, this guy has a pair of breasts that would send many women screaming into the streets in search of a good implant surgeon.

Have you seen this guy? At first I didn't believe it. From the waist up, I thought somebody had stuck Ilie Nastase's face on Heather Locklear's body.

Fabio, the man of the nineties. This must be what women want, they're flocking to him by the millions.

And, in our unending quest to become what women want, we middle-aged stupid straight guys must now emulate and imitate Fabio as much as possible. But don't get too close to him. If he gets just a fraction more nurturing, I'm pretty sure this guy's going to lactate.

Okay, I said it. I'm sorry.

Sex – Have We Covered
All the Bases Yet?

As the official spokesman for the Middle-Aged Stupid Straight
Guy Association, I am both appalled and angered by all the
fuss being made about same-sex marriages.

I mean, have these people been living on the planet Pluto for
the past twenty years or what?

For gawdsakes, wake up and smell the aphrodisiacs. There are
sex therapy clinics, there are sex manuals, there are self-help
videos and consultants like Dr. Ruth Westheimer, there are weekend retreats and seminars designed to put the spark back into the
marriage and enhance the physical relationship.

In this day and age, there's no reason in the world why sex in
the marriage always has to be the same.

And now they're even proposing legislation to recognize that
sex must be the same. This is ridiculous! I was married once, I
can recognize boring sex a mile away! And another thing . . .

What? Excuse me one second . . . it's not? *What!? You're Kidding!? Why?? Who?? Whoaaa!!!*

Sorry, but I have just been informed by my editor that I may not have completely understood the concept of same-sex marriage.

For members of the Middle-Aged Stupid Straight Guy Association, it's like a two-mommy marriage as opposed to, but in conjunction with, a two-daddy marriage.

Boy, all this stuff is going by me so fast, numbered jerseys and a program of players probably wouldn't help at this point.

I'm about as confused as a kid of a same-sex marriage who wins a newspaper contest with the essay "Why My Mom Is the Greatest Dad in the World!" You think the average kid is a little confused now, just wait until he goes to his father to ask where babies come from and he's told to go ask his father.

It shouldn't be quite this complicated. It should be like the old days: it should be almost as simple as getting a summer softball game going.

"Okay, heterosexuals on this team, homosexuals over there. We'll flip a coin to see who bats first. Everybody knows the rules — nine innings, three strikes and you're out, and of course you walk if you have four . . . well, everybody knows the rules. Okay, any questions?

"Yeah? You're bisexual? Okay, no problem. What? No, no. You're not going to bat for both teams. Yes, I'm well aware of the fact that you can swing from both sides of the plate, but you have to go out in the field and chase grounders like everybody else.

"Yes, you, sir? You want to play right field hard and aggressive like Joe Carter? That's fine. But you want to wear a ballerina's outfit with full facial make-up? Sure, okay. But take the spiked heels off. This is just a friendly pick-up game.

"You, sir? Sorry. You, ma'am? Sorry. You? Oh, you're asexual. And that means . . . okay, gotcha. So you have no interest in either team or even the game itself but you do want to be a part of it all. Okay. That's fair. Perhaps just sitting on the sidelines and observing . . . as a kind of disinterested, unbiased cheerleader? Good.

"And you? You are a hermaphrodite? And that means? You're kidding. No, no, actually I knew that. Okay, so you would have a handle on . . . you would have a fair idea of how both teams play. Okay then, how about umpiring? Sure, we can get you two chest protectors.

"Okay, is that pretty much it?

"Yes, you, sir. Oh, sorry. You, ma'am. So last season you were a *he* and this season you're a *she*. Well, that's okay — we don't have to know the details. Oh, you have a protective cup you want to sell. Perhaps there's somebody here who recently changed the other way around? There you go — the guy in the culottes over there.

"Okay now, is that about it?

"Yes, you, sir. You're confused, you're getting cranky, you just came to play softball, and the sun is going down already. Sir, you can be the captain of my team."

There was a time when I kind of liked that old expression used to describe a total incompetent: "Couldn't organize sex in a bordello." Unfortunately, it just ain't that easy anymore.

Fair warning: If you are of a new sex or you have invented a new sex or you prefer from-another-planet sex — I urge you to go public and get it on the record now. We've gotta close this thing off pretty soon.

Buffalo, New York
– City Under the Big Top

I quite like the city of Buffalo — its chicken wings, its clam bars, and, above all, its Grand Canyon-style potholes which U.S. archaeologists believe to be air holes used to ventilate the lost continent of Atlantis, now resurfaced under the assumed name of Cheektowaga, with no known survivors.

If you're a Buffalo-watcher as I am, you come to understand that the three fastest-growing groups of people in that city are Canadians coming over to buy their own beer back, weird people behind the wheels of cars, and very bad bank robbers.

Buffalo is known as a city with heart, and it is with this in mind that I would like to dedicate this piece to the conscientious people of that city, who have a healthier respect for drinking and driving laws than any other city in America, indeed the world.

Buffalo citizens so rigorously, so relentlessly, so religiously refuse to drink and drive that they will actually . . . well, let's go to the police blotter to see firsthand how far they're willing to go.

111

Quoting from the first news report: "Kevin Ford and Donald McNair were charged with various driving-related offenses in June in Buffalo, N.Y., after Ford's brother Montgomery drove Kevin's car up a utility pole guide wire, causing the car to flip over. Kevin explained that he had been drinking and turned the keys over to Montgomery, who is blind, but who 'always wanted to drive.'"

Well, far be it from me to stand in the way of another man's dream, but I think letting blind people operate moving vehicles, no matter how good the verbal communication skills of the drunk in the passenger seat, is a very bad idea.

For one thing, you cannot pass by a blind driver, point at his flat tire, and hope he responds accordingly.

To my knowledge, driving by touch has never proven to be a good idea, insurance-wise. Plus it can be downright dangerous.

And it can be especially dangerous when you consider there could be young children out on those Buffalo streets . . . also operating motor vehicles.

Back to the police blotter for last week's item: "A city of Tonawanda woman was arrested Friday after police said she had her 11-year-old niece take the wheel of her car because she was too drunk to drive." Deborah Hallam, thirty-eight, apparently decided she'd had a few too many and instructed her niece, whom she was baby-sitting at the time, how to drive the car. (Boy, this must be the accelerated version of Young Drivers of America.)

At one a.m., Officer Robert Clontz spotted the car driving erratically down Delaware Street where it nearly struck a utility pole. (One a.m.? I suppose now that they have the kid up on a dangerous driving rap, they're willing to overlook the fact that she was up past her bedtime.)

I'm all for teaching children to master skills of dexterity early in life, and driving may be one of them, but certainly not

112

in a city where blind people are prone to make lane changes without signalling.

I feel Buffalo, New York, simply has no choice in these matters. They must crack down now, restore safety rules to city streets, and once and for all — get rid of all utility poles within city limits! That, and publish a very strict list entitled: No Matter How Drunk You Are — Never Give Your Car Keys To:

- Blind people, including those with a highly developed sense of hearing.
- Any person who can still travel free on airlines by sitting in a parent's lap.
- Inanimate objects.
- Iraqis who hold grudges.
- Any cat under four foot two and not in possession of a valid New York State driver's licence.
- People on the thruway driving alongside you.
- Dead people, even those still able to sit up and grip things.
- People who become life-like only when you inflate with an air hose.
- Real buffalo, including those who made cameo appearances in *Dancing with Wolves*.
- Imaginary or invisible friends.

It's a pretty safe bet that our own symbol of safety, Elmer the Safety Elephant, would not only be a popular cartoon figure in Buffalo, he'd also be a much-sought-after designated driver.

If you drive in Buffalo, please show compassion for blind guys and small children by giving them very clear and helpful driving tips like: "Holy #%@! You just missed that utility pole!"

Among bank robbers across America, Buffalo is affectionately known as the Home of the Exploding Dye Pack.

Yet it doesn't seem to matter. A recent study released in Buffalo revealed that, although more and more people are seeking employment as full-time bank robbers, eighty percent of them are always getting caught. This explains why police in that city are constantly on the lookout for fugitives described as "armed and stupid."

So back to that ever-expanding police blotter for the story of Cylester Arrington. On January 19 of this year, Cy, all jumped up on cocaine and wearing no disguise whatsoever, walked into the Chase Bank of Broadway Avenue and made, in criminal vernacular, one boner of a butt-head blunder.

That was his first mistake, showing up. Then Cy said hello to the bank security guard, described in the police report as "an old family friend."

Okay, so Cy scores big points for politeness.

Next, Cy walked up to the teller and demanded cash while menacingly holding a finger in his pocket as if it were a gun. The teller, who was not so much traumatized as she was trying to stifle a laugh, handed Cy a bundle of cash which immediately exploded, covering him in red dye.

And then Cy, standing there dripping in red indelible ink, did something that will eventually put him in The Stupid Bank Robbers Hall of Fame. Cy grabbed a nearby customer and pointed his pretend gun (i.e., the index finger of his right hand) at the customer's neck and demanded they be allowed to walk out of the bank.

Please note. Cy did not say: "We both walk out of here or I'll pop every blackhead in this guy's neck!" No, I just made that up.

What Cy did was stand there holding the hostage until that old family friend came over and whacked him over the head approximately six times with a night stick. This, in effect, put an end to the robbery before Cy could threaten to blow up the manager's office with a chunk of Bazooka Bubble Gum. Although Cy was

114

arrested and subsequently convicted, he was voted Mr. Congeniality by the Greater Buffalo Police Association.

So, not only is Cy Arrington now doing five years in a federal penitentiary, his family and the bank guard's family are no longer on speaking terms.

And isn't that the tragedy of crime — it's the families who suffer the most.

Buffalo, New York — in much more need of a ringmaster than a mayor.

The Mary Kay of Sunset Bay

Every community has a kid like Kelly Beck.

Kelly is seven years old with long blonde hair and shy hazel eyes, and this kid could sell exercise bikes to the recently deceased.

Kelly is the neighbourhood salesperson. While other children are trading baseball cards and Barbie clothes, Kelly is going door-to-door in my Sunset Bay neighbourhood, sending her prospective customers scurrying for crawl spaces with handfuls of Extra Strength Tylenol.

It's not so much what she's selling, because quite often Kelly's not really sure. In fact, for a while Kelly had an older girl working with her door-to-door. This was before Kelly could talk. When Kelly was old enough to talk, she told me the older girl's name was District Sales Manager. As soon as Kelly developed a vocabulary of twenty words, she fired the District Sales Manager.

Kelly now affectionately refers to her house as the Home Office, her brothers and sisters as Account Executives, and the yellow school bus as the Company Car.

Kelly's so smooth she doesn't even bring the product around with her anymore. She carries an order form headed "Ja Want Sum?" and a pen. That's it. A great salesperson, as Kelly says, doesn't need product — "Thell the thizzle, not the thteak!"

I know, I'm her best customer. Even if I were her only customer, Kelly Beck would have made more in commissions last year than the guy with exclusive sales rights to car phones in Mississauga. (I know as soon as her mother reads this to her, I'll be sorry for mentioning car phones.)

Kelly Beck is the princess of pitch. Her weak, almost inaudible knock at the door says: "I'm embarrassed to be here, and I'm sorry to bother you, but two slathering Rottweilers and a hailstorm aren't going to move me away from this door so get out here. I don't have all day!"

Once you open the door, you're done. Kelly shifts from one foot to the other, locks those pretty-please eyes on you, thrusts the pen and paper toward you, and without mentioning what she's selling, says: "Ja want sum?" The choice is clear: Sign or be guilty of cruelty to second-graders working their way through Wainfleet South Elementary School. It's easier to say "no" to Revenue Canada than to Kelly Beck, the Mary Kay of Sunset Bay. You sigh, you surrender, you sign.

I've got jars full of Girl Guide cookies, a refrigerator full of cheese, and enough tickets of chance to warrant a gaming licence. I've sponsored Kelly Beck in so many Walk-a-thons, Swim-a-thons, Bowl-a-thons, Bike-a-thons, Stand-a-thons, Sleep-over-a-thons, and Whistle-while-you-work-a-thons, she ought to legally have her name changed to "The Bionic Beck."

I've got so many magnetic note pads on my refrigerator, the other day my lawn mower entered the house all by itself.

Last week she was back. Kelly did the sales shuffle, locked in the eyes, pushed the pen and paper at me, and said: "Ja want sum?" I signed. But being an educated consumer, I forced myself to ask: "What did I just buy?"

"Macramé," she said with the smile of success and batting her eyes to boot. Great. An afghan or a wall hanging. Either way, I'd give it to my mom for Christmas.

When UPS delivered the microwave with three-stage memory and automatic thaw, I was steamed.

When Kelly showed up at my door the next day, I was still livid. I lit into her . . . but then she handed me Madame Benoit's *Illustrated Encyclopedia of Microwave Cooking*. "It's free — with the macramé," she said.

Then she started to shift her feet. Gawd no, not the sales shift . . . not the eyes, not the pen, here it comes: "Ja want sum?"

"Okay," I said signing, "but this better not be a household appliance or a Walk-a-thon along the Great Wall of China."

"It's not," she replied. "It's a blayther."

Hmmm . . . a blazer. Looks like I got off easy this time.

She was two doors down when it dawned on me.

"How do you know the right size?" I yelled.

"It's a four-by-four Chevrolet Blayther — fully loaded with cruwth contwol," she yelled back, while knocking on the Tryfiaks' door. I watched as John and Diane jumped out of their bedroom window and ran down the beach toward Morgan's Point.

I know this kid has got to be stopped, but I couldn't help but wonder: Does "fully loaded" include a CD player with a six-cassette loading cartridge, or what?

And That's Why I Love
Small Town Living

It had to happen sooner or later.

You cannot live in rural and small town Canada without eventually being stained by the splash of big city crime.

The sad fact is that the small town of Port Colborne, a few miles down Lakeshore Road from me, just had its very first, its very own gunman/hostage-taking/standoff.

How small is Port Colborne, Ontario? Well, it's so small that the gunman couldn't get his hands on a victim so he took himself hostage.

This is good news for family, friends, and neighbours; this is bad news for your home-alone gunman.

You see, and I believe the experts will back me up on this one, in a prolonged process of negotiation, a gunman without a hostage has severely limited his bargaining power.

For instance, when a gunman comes out to make his break, holds the gun to his own head, and yells: "Cash and a car or I'm gonna pop this guy!" every emergency task force team in Canada is trained to stand down and let this problem pretty much take care of itself.

And, after two or three or four days, a gunman without a hostage really has no one to trade for coffee and sandwiches.

For me, it just doesn't work. No, for me a hostage-taker without a hostage is like a drive-by shooter on an exercise bike.

The incident in Port Colborne began when the roof of the gunman's apartment began leaking and he fired off several shots. I know what you're thinking — a lot of guys would have just called a plumber. Well, let's not be too hasty here. How many times have you banged on the top of the television set before finally phoning the repairman? That's how these human tragedies happen. One day you're tapping the glass on your VCR where "12:00" has been flashing since the day you bought the damn thing, the next day you're dropping torpedoes down the toilet.

Anyway, the police were summoned, and the gunman settled in for the siege with a 30/30 rifle, a shotgun, a club, a hunting knife, a machete, and a bow with arrows. Basically he was better armed than the Canadian forces we had in Bosnia but not quite as well protected as a tour-bus driver in Miami.

During the thirty-one-hour standoff that followed, the police tried to call the gunman to negotiate an end to it all, but as luck would have it, the guy did not have a phone. This was a real shock to residents out here in Wainfleet who already have call waiting.

At some point the police sent Freebee, their Remote Mobile Investigative Unit, into the apartment and the gunman shot the hell out of the robot. This was a big mistake. I'm no expert in this area, but couldn't Freebee have become the hostage he never had? Think about it — not only is that thing very expensive to replace, if it's as smart as the cops claim it is, the robot could have driven the gunman's getaway car.

Anyway, the good news is that Freebee is not dead. He's listed in fair condition in the Intensive Care Unit at Atlas Steels in Welland.

At precisely 4:06 p.m. on the second day of the standoff, the Niagara Regional Police Emergency Task Force Unit said enough is enough and began what they call their "tear gas campaign." They lobbed over a dozen tear gas cannisters at the windows of the gunman's apartment. Unfortunately, every one of them missed the window and bounced off the side of the building. Twelve misses in a row? That's not a "tear gas campaign," I believe that's Kim Campbell's campaign!

121

When the police finally did get one into the apartment, the gunman picked it up and threw it back out the window.

It was fortunate that all his neighbours in the building, who had been evacuated, didn't run back up the stairs and into the gunman's apartment — at this point, the only place in the neighbourhood with clean air.

I counted eighteen softball-sized pockmarks on the side of the building where the tear gas cannisters bounced off. One such dent was two feet off the ground. The gunman's apartment was on the second floor. Either the police assumed he had a midget accomplice or they just gotta straighten out the barrel of that tear gas gun.

Anyway, the gunman gave himself up. I don't know if it was the tear gas or the fear of losing his damage deposit. Personally, I think he just couldn't stand the brutal beating the vinyl siding was taking.

And that's why I love small town living. Because even in the throes of a real live hostage-taking standoff, neither the criminal nor the cops pose a threat to public safety.

IV

Guys Setting Off the Jerk Detector

Dinner with Danny

A while back, a Toronto therapist was quoted as saying: "Men often experience deep, loving feelings about other males, but most find it hard to show how much they really care. By contrast, they usually have no problem kissing and hugging women, or telling them I love you."

This is a therapist who's been spending way too much time in Support Group City.

Frankly, I'm appalled. I know guys and I don't know one who doesn't have a problem kissing and hugging a woman and telling her he loves her unless: (a) the room has already been paid for, or (b) the wedding cake is about to be cut and he doesn't want to disappoint the relatives who drove all the way from South Porcupine.

As for the yucky stuff about men showing other men about how much they care, I'd like to advise the therapist — get real, go attend a John Wayne film festival, go join a full-contact street-hockey league that plays forty home games on Yonge Street south of Bloor.

Good Lord — most guys need three drinks to say "I love you" to their mothers on Mother's Day.

You see, guys adhere to Rule #1 of Relationships: "The first one to say I love you — loses." For example, if a guy tells a woman I love you, and she confesses that rather than say I love you back she'd rather have her nose pierced and hang a cow bell from her face for the rest of her natural life — the man is branded as a jerk. He's beat. About the only thing he can do to recover from such an ego-thrashing is to give himself a whole hive of hickies and go down to the pub and tell lies about that tramp.

On the other hand, if the woman says "I love you," then the guy can honestly reply with what comes naturally to all sensitive, caring males: "So you wanna go bowl a few frames?" Then on the way to Bowl-O-Rama he can point out the relatively insignificant difference between renting bowling shoes or a suite at Journey's End.

From the male standpoint, this is a win-win situation. At best, you get lucky, get married, and start a family of your own. At worst, you get to go bowling.

This is the way male-initiated relationships have worked since the beginning of time.

Then, instead of charm men used clubs, instead of hotel suites they used caves, and instead of bowling they curled — but really, little else has changed.

So, if the modern male has evolved from primeval apes to his present emotionally impaired form, incapable of expressing his innermost feelings to a woman, I'm sorry but I just don't see him saying "I love you" to the guy he's been going duck hunting with for the last twenty years.

Let me describe to you what happens when a guy shows affection for another guy. Let us call this little vignette *Dinner with Danny*.

Occasionally, I get together and have dinner with my brother-in-law Danny, who is a postie but in many other ways self-respecting and aware of the changes of seasons. I was married once. She got the '68 Cutlass convertible, and I got stuck with the cat and her brother. Both need a lot of looking after.

I like Danny. Danny likes me. But we don't go carving our initials in tree trunks for the whole freakin' world to see. That's the beauty of guys, eh?

On this night, Danny bought the steaks and iced the beer and we watched *Cheers*, Danny's last connection with what Freud described as "human reality." I did the cooking.

When *Cheers* ended, Danny threw a Leonard Cohen disc on the compact disc player and we sat down to eat at a very small kitchen table separated only by garlic bread and bottles of imported beer. Danny's apartment is the second floor of an old house; it's badly lit with wide-open stairs winding up from the front porch.

Halfway through dinner we hear a faint knock, the clump of footsteps, and two guys that play on Danny's baseball team walk in.

It was just after Danny gave them each a beer and they sat with their mouths open not pouring anything in, that my brother-in-law and I said to ourselves, What's wrong with this picture? Two guys having dinner that isn't Chinese take-out, drinks, dim lighting, and Leonard Cohen belting out "Ain't No Cure for Love."

It must have looked like Harvey Fierstein's adaptation of *The Odd Couple*.

It could have been worse only if we'd have been dancing between courses.

As Leonard Cohen launched into "I'm Your Man," a nervous voice from across the room asked: "So whatter you guys up to?"

"We're planning our trip together," replied Danny.

Now for all intents and purposes, we might as well have been dancing between courses.

It was true, we were driving down to Florida to play tennis the following week.

"Yup," I added in my best John Wayne voice. "We're going up to Haliburton to shoot bears in the town dump!"

Danny, who knows I couldn't kill a mouse if I caught it eating my royalty cheque, jumped in quick: "Yeah, and we got babes lined up along the way, too!"

The testosterone level was rising so fast we both experienced an urge to do "high fives" and butt heads.

"Yup," I said, "bears, babes, and I don't care what the warning label on the pack says, we're gonna start smoking Camels too!"

A shrill whine erupted from the overhead fan. The worst had happened. We had activated the Jerk Detector.

That's when Danny's friends got up and silently left without touching their beer.

And that's what happens when guys show affection to guys.

Danny yelled down the stairs: "You wanna tag-team arm wrestle for the empties?" But they were long gone.

Rule #2 of Relationships: *The Dinner with Danny* addendum. If you want to have dinner with another guy, make sure it's McDonald's where you can make sexist remarks about the girls behind the counter and punch each other in the arm a lot. Wearing camouflage clothing and cleaning your fingers with jackknives wouldn't hurt neither. (Neither: Non-affectionate guys can use that word anywhere they want in a sentence.)

Never Go Canoeing
in Hurricane Hugo

G oing on a canoe trip with your accountant can be as much fun as discussing old rocks with a paleontologist who doesn't drink.

But this trip promised to be different. We were going in late September to gaze in wonderment and capture on film the annual classic changing of the colours, deep in Algonquin Park. You have to wonder about the excitement level of a society which, in great numbers, migrates north each fall to witness leaves dying.

The first night, Thursday, was so absolutely perfect we didn't bother putting up a tent. We slept in sleeping bags under a star-studded sky, with warm breezes teasing a sparkling fire well into the night. After a candle-lit meal of pan-fried steaks with red wine followed by cigars and brandy, I swear if we'd had a tape of John Denver's "Rocky Mountain High," somebody would have been ordering out for an engagement ring.

Oh, and did I mention the accountant brought his dog along? That's correct. Now a lot of guys wouldn't do that. But then again a lot of guys wouldn't go camping with their accountant, so he's not the only one here who's not all that smart.

So, as we marvelled at the hushed serenity of nature's wilderness, Lady, a two-year-old yellow retriever, whose brain is in the mail, treed every raccoon from Lake Opeongo to the city limits of Schumacher.

Friday was wet and dreary, but we plunged on after assurances from the lady at the Natural Resources office in Opeongo that it would clear up. She's a very nice woman, but could we all just take a solemn moment here and pray to God she never becomes a TV weatherperson? Because on Friday night, Hugo dropped by our campsite. That would be the tail-end of Hurricane Hugo, and he arrived at about ten o'clock in the evening.

The wind-driven rain pierced the tent, the tent floor, and the sleeping bags. We slept in four inches of water and I'm not exaggerating. When one of us turned over in a sleeping bag, both of us could feel and hear the four-inch wave slosh from side to side in the tent.

But experts will tell you that man can survive all night lying in a wading pool, unless of course the temperature drops to the freezing point, which it did at precisely 12:02 a.m. The accountant had a watch. What we desperately needed was a rescue flare gun, and I'm stranded with a guy who can't stop admiring his new Rolex.

Faced with freezing to death in a bush, twenty-one miles from civilization, a very strange thing happens. The value of the dog rises exponentially with the decreasing degrees of temperature. For the record, she was sleeping on my feet before the freeze hit. The accountant then lured her over to his side of the tent with a promise of doggie treats, which, unbeknownst to him, I had already eaten once I realized only one of us might live to tell this story.

After a brief rendition of that classic Paul McCartney/Michael Jackson collaboration — "The doggone girl is mine, no she isn't, yes she is, no she isn't, yes she is!" — we compromised and placed the dog between us at the head of the tent. Fortunately, her face fell to my side where I basked in the warmth of her breath, a courageous feat on my part since this dog, more than any dog I've ever been that close to, really could have used a mint.

You have to remember that the whole trip was the accountant's idea so whatever warm air he was basking in at the other end — I figured he deserved.

Now we're soaked and freezing and waiting and praying for the first light of dawn. I'm convinced if we can make it to morning we will somehow escape or at least die with other campers. So I'm pretending that this horrible night is moving right along when the accountant says: "Guess what time it is?"

I knew I had an hour of life left in me, so I ignored him and pretended to be asleep.

"It's only five after one," he said, adding, "I thought it might be later."

I wondered if there was a chapter in the *Happy Camper's Guide to Canoeing with an Accountant* under mercy killing?

Judge: "So he kept reminding you of how slowly the time was passing?"
Me: "Every two minutes, your Honour."
Judge: "So you suffocated him with a . . . a . . ."
Me: "A golden retriever, sir."
Judge: "And what did he do for a living?"
Me: "He was an accountant."
Judge: "Case dismissed."

It had become apparent that we were being buried and frozen alive in a barren trap, so desolate, so bleak, so absolutely hopeless that only Kim Campbell's political strategist had been there before. When I stopped shivering long enough to hear the dog's teeth chatter, I knew it was the end of the line.

"That's it," I said. "I'm out."

And off we went into the night to the other side of the island where we stumbled into the camp of two guys from Ottawa. With a system of tarps and common sense, these guys had managed to stay dry and keep a fire going. These guys were smart. They were also men who were capable of pitying beings of a lesser biological order.

To Don Drew and Geraint Lewis, I thank you for saving the lives of two friends who will be ever grateful and indebted to you. Why you bothered saving the accountant too, Lady and I will never understand.

Oh, and did I mention that the next day the winds got up to 60 mph and it snowed? All we needed was hail and a plague of locusts to hit for the complete cycle of natural disasters.

Thereafter, we spent two full days and nights hovering like sausages over an open fire.

We allowed ourselves to be lured away from the flames only by a rescue boat from the Ministry of Natural Resources.

I'll never go canoeing with my accountant again, but I sure hope he'll let me borrow his dog.

Sexual Harassment
– A Guide for Men

The United States Senate confirmation hearings of Clarence Thomas's nomination to the Supreme Court riveted North America to the television set like nothing since the Persian Gulf War. And once again the ones who wore robes lost.

I don't know about you but any inquiry into sexual misconduct that puts a Kennedy on the side of the investigators has enough dramatic irony to hook me on daytime TV.

I'm always shocked by any disgraceful television broadcast of crude and lewd sexual behaviour which does not have Geraldo Rivera as its host.

These dramatic and titillating escapades broadcast live on all three major television networks represented television at its best — reaping high drama from low moral fibre.

It was astounding to me that the majority of Americans, both senators and citizens, did not believe Anita Hill, an articulate and intelligent law professor, who had nothing to gain by her painful testimony and a whole lot to lose.

However, if you remember that this is a nation which also believed Iraq had the fourth largest army in the world, Oliver North was/is a hero, and Richard Nixon's only sin was getting caught — well, it makes it a little easier to understand.

Sexual harassment in the workplace — men talking dirty at the water cooler, patting bums, and brushing up against breasts, and women even extorting sex from men who work under them — wow! It's a little disconcerting to learn that we're in the worst recession in sixty years because everybody in the workplace is hitting on each other, eight hours a day.

Can you imagine all the guys who work in a plant who would have been taking night courses in business management if they had known there was so much action going on in the office? I mean, who knew?

Reading the details of sexual harassment cases splashed across the pages of every North American newspaper these past three weeks makes you wonder why anybody would actually leave work to go to a singles bar.

Working at home as I have for the past thirteen years, I can't remember exactly when the common company office turned into Plato's Retreat.

Yet sexual harassment remains a real problem, and as an objective observer, I feel I am in a good position to set down a few guidelines for men to keep them on the "straight and narrow" while at work.

Ten Tips for a Sex-Free Workplace

TIP #1 — Men, if the combination of black stockings and a black push-up bra makes you aroused and uncontrollable — then for gawdsakes, stop wearing them!

TIP #2 — The next time you want to discuss the best parts of the porno flick you saw last night, make sure you're speaking in a very low voice, in a remote area of the building, to Carl the company custodian.

TIP #3 — Boorish, foul-mouthed, and lewd language will no longer be tolerated in any Canadian workplace except of course the House of Commons.

TIP #4 — Effective immediately, office party favours will go back to being stupid hats and paper crackers.

TIP #5 — Innuendo, double-entendres, and sexually ambiguous talk will be restricted to lawyers' offices where nobody gets them anyway.

TIP #6 — If you say "I'd love to see what's under that!" make sure you're pointing to the dust cover of the new fax machine.

TIP #7 — Cat-calls and wolf-whistles are permissible only if a member of each of these species is in the room at the time.

TIP #8 — If you say "What a great pair of headlights!" make sure you are able to see the parking lot from your office window.

TIP #9 — Before you come up behind a female co-worker and give her a hug, make certain she's choking on food.

Yes, the jig is up, boys. It will come as a shock to many of you, but from here on in, the workplace is a place to work.

TIP #10 — And remember (this one could save your livelihood): the next time you're tempted to pat a bum, imagine your own in a vice.

Let's Just Leave It Alone

In the last six months, it would seem that North American males have made an incredible and somewhat painful discovery — their main private part.

You may recall the incident in Manassas, Virginia, in which John Wayne Bobbitt's wife cut off his gillooly. In July in Waynesville, North Carolina, Cynthia Gillett set her husband's on fire. Last spring, José Dogelio had his shot by a woman in Dasmarinas, Philippines, whom he was flashing at the time. And in Ransomville, New York, during July 4 celebration a twenty-eight-year-old man was injured when a firecracker bounced back up from the ground and lodged in his shorts before exploding.

Who knew that in the grotesque decade we've come to know as the nineties, the neighbourhood most men want to rid of violence, stabbings, and shootings is the one between the two front pockets of their jeans.

The most sensational case was that of John Wayne Bobbitt, who suffered the double indignity of first having it sliced off and then having it thrown out the window of a car by his wife.

My first question was, What did the cops who went looking for it say when asked by a passerby what they were doing?

"Ah, we're looking for John Wayne Bobbitt's thingamajig here. Have you seen it? It's about yay big and answers to the name of John Wayne Junior."

A second question came to mind after the surgeon who successfully performed the reattachment stated at a news conference: "I expect all major functions to eventually return."

All? *All!?* I know of two major functions. Are there a lot of other things, recreational or otherwise, I could have been doing with this thing that I didn't know about? I mean, are there guys out there putting it in a slip knot and waterskiing behind boats, or using it to lasso Brahma bulls?

I knew a guy in college who put a tiny toque on his and used it as the dummy in his ventriloquist act, but that was it.

I'm forty-seven years of age, and if there are a lot of other uses for this thing, I think I have a right to know. Now!

Of course, we have in Canada a Toronto surgeon just back from China with a technique he claims can lengthen a man's penis by fifty percent. The procedure, which costs $3,000, is not covered by provincial health plans and apparently involves neither the relocation of a finger, nor Krazy Glue.

We've all heard the names of the principals involved in this operation. The Toronto surgeon is Dr. Stubbs, who learned the procedure from China's Dr. Long. The man who originally developed the technique is from Beijing, and his name is Dr. Dong. This is apparently all true.

However, if I find out former federal minister Gerry Weiner or New York Mayor David Dinkins has anything to do with this, I'm going to call for a public inquiry into the whole affair, headed by Ben Wicks.

Now I'm not pointing a . . . I'm not blaming anybody for all this sudden and unsubtle interest in man's second-best friend, but it seems to me it all began with the release of the movie *Free Willy*. Coincidence? I don't think so.

No matter who started it all, it just naturally has to stop.

We need a national policy, indeed an international policy, on the future of the male member. I mean are we making it bigger just so it's an easier target for those who want to stab it, shoot it, set it on fire, and use it as a sparkler on the Fourth of July?

I, for one, will not stand by idly as this former vital organ is trivialized. I never want to turn on the television and see Cy Sperling saying, "I'm not only the Hair Club president, but here's my new member!"

No, this has to stop and soon.

I am absolutely appalled that a licenced surgeon of Dr. Stubbs's stature and a member of the College of Physicians would stoop so low as to make stupid little dinky jokes about male genitalia when, in fact, I believe that's my job.

I want this stopped now, and I'll tell you how we're going to do it.

We're going to run a series of national television ads urging Canadians to restore privacy to the male private part. These ads will star my eighty-seven-year-old mother. Marg will stand in front of the camera, look every male Canadian over the age of puberty straight in the eye, and say:

"You keep fiddling with that thing and you're going to poke somebody's eye out."

Hey, it worked for me.

Hey! You Got a Licence to Fly That Lawn Chair?

A llow me to introduce you to my Man of the Year. For sheer brilliance of mind, for complete wisdom in thought, and for absolute physical control of the human body — well, you'll have to find your own Man of the Year.

Me? I picked Larry Walters of North Hollywood, California. Larry Walters went where no man has ever dared to go before, not in a lawn chair anyway.

Larry is my kind of guy, because Larry accepted the challenge of the human spirit and although, as any woman could have predicted, he did screw up big time — Larry did not die.

As our story unfolds in a backyard near the Pacific Ocean, not dying slowly but surely becomes Larry's goal in life.

Larry Walters, with no apparent help from mind-altering drugs or even a rap on the noggin with a blunt instrument, experienced a "Peter Pan-style dream to hook himself to a bundle of balloons and float high past the sprawling Los Angeles metropolis into the desert beyond."

Well, not to question Larry's sense of originality, but I think this is the dream of every man, every man who wears leotards that are way too tight. So he did what any man would do who hears the voice: "If you build it, they will come!" Only thing is, Larry had no idea "they" referred to case-workers in the field of mental health.

So Larry built his dream ship and it consisted of a fold-up aluminum lawn chair attached to forty-two helium-filled weather balloons and a bunch of milk jugs filled with water for ballast. Simple by design, Larry's home-made dirigible had going-up power, going-down power, and a lawn chair where a cockpit might normally be.

Larry's on-board equipment consisted of a two-way radio, an altimeter, a wristwatch, and a pellet pistol. Because he lacked an overhead compartment or any space under the seat in front of him, Larry's aviation tools were selected for their ability to fit in his pants pockets.

I know what you're asking yourself — what the hell was the wristwatch for? Well, that was so Larry could make it home in time for supper after his inaugural flight.

The purpose of the pellet gun was to shoot out the weather balloons in the event Larry had to bring that baby down in a hurry.

Now this may have been the end of the story except that Larry was doing a manned rehearsal of his craft in his girlfriend's backyard in nearby San Pedro, when he noticed the ropes he had secured to the eavestroughs of the house had been rubbing against the sharp metal edge and — *whoaaaaa!* Larry Walters hurled himself into the space age a little prematurely.

Luckily, that lawn chair had armrests you could really grab onto because the helium had Larry rising faster than the Spaceship Columbia at Launch +10.

Not one but two (and oh, how I hoped to get through this story without saying "I'm not making this up") commercial airline pilots from Delta and TWA reported to the control tower the sighting of a man in a lawn chair airborne over L.A. International Airport.

Drug-testing being what it is in the airline industry, I don't think any of us can imagine the courage it took these pilots to make those calls. Had a passenger made the spotting, you can be sure those tiny airline liquor bottles would be the first to go under lock and key.

At 16,000 feet and still rising, and getting dizzy in the cold thin air, Larry began shooting out the weather balloons with his pellet gun. His theory worked only too well, and he came down out of the sky faster than . . . well . . . a guy strapped in a lawn chair and attached to a lot of milk jugs filled with water.

He was headed for a crash landing on a golf course until the balloons' tethers wrapped themselves around high-voltage lines near the airport. Larry, as the miracle goes, was rescued.

He has since appeared in magazine ads for Timex, the maker of the wristwatch he was wearing during his flight. There's no doubt in my mind, that Larry's Timex is still ticking but his brain has been flashing "12:00" for a very long time.

He was reportedly paid $1,000 for the Timex ad but fined $1,500 by the United States Federal Aviation Administration for entering international airspace without an airplane. Gee, I wish Larry had called me first. We could have tied two lawn chairs side by side, I could have brought along one of those Super Soaker water pistols, and we could have scared the hell out of stewardesses all up and down the California coast.

My Man of the Year — free-falling from 16,000 feet in a lawn chair — guys like Larry don't fold.

Sergei Krikalev, Don't Call Home

The fall of the Berlin Wall caught us all by surprise, but nobody's lower lip dropped further than that of Sergei Krikalev. Sergei was the forty-nine-year-old Russian cosmonaut who was circling the earth in a spaceship when the Brandenburg Gate blew open. With the immediate disintegration of the Soviet Union, Sergei was left in weightless limbo for 280 days until the Russians could figure out a way to get him down. Not only was there a problem of money in the space program, the former Soviet launch site was now in a foreign country.

When Sergei and his Soyuz rocket were shot into space, the cosmonaut had a pretty good handle on life as well as a homeland to return to. Now, less than a year later there's no Soviet Union, and an awful lot has changed.

Can you imagine the conversation between poor Sergei, the circling jerk, and the guy at ground control who has to guide him down?

Sergei: "Okay, I've almost completed programming for re-entry but usually I line up my visual flight path with the Great Wall of China, then the Matterhorn, and then . . . where's the Berlin Wall?"

Ground control: "Gone."

Sergei: "Where did it go?"

Ground control: "Most of it went to the United States where it sold for $50 an ounce."

Sergei: "They are smoking the Berlin Wall in the United States! What kind of country is dis?"

Ground control: "No, Sergei, souvenirs of communism."

Sergei: "Where is communism?"

Ground control: "Now exclusively in Cuba. Look Sergei, we don't have a lot of time so . . . "

Sergei: "Will you please call my family in Leningrad and tell them I'll be home soon?"

Ground control: "Ah, Sergei, I don't know how to tell you this, but Leningrad doesn't exist any more."

Sergei: "You mean Leningrad was blown off the face of the earth in a nuclear disaster?"

Ground control: "No, that was Chernobyl. Sergei, have you got your oxygen valve turned all the way up?"

Sergei: "I knew about Chernobyl. Where's my family?"

Ground control: "St. Petersburg."

Sergei: "The Berlin Wall went to the United States and my family moved to Florida?"

Ground control: "They changed the name from Leningrad to St. Petersburg."

Sergei: "Lenin must be turning over in his grave."

Ground control: "Actually, they're thinking of selling Lenin."

Sergei: "Let me guess . . . to the United States?"

Ground control: "Affirmative, Sergei. Another souvenir of communism."

At this point Sergei Krikalev rolls his eyes, which is really neat because in the weightlessness of outer space they actually go all the way around.

Ground control: "Now, Sergei, when you land in Kazakhstan be sure to . . . "

Sergei: "Did you say Pakistan?"

Ground control: "Kazakhstan."

Sergei: "Where is that?"

Ground control: "It's north of Tadzhikistan and Turkmenistan, sharing a border with Uzbekistan."

Sergei: "Are those countries or kiosks?"

Ground control: "Hey, Sergei, don't be a Yakov Smirnoff, eh? I'm just doing my job here."

Sergei: "I thought I was coming home to the motherland of Russia."

Ground control: "Sorry, did you say Russia or Byelorussia?"

Sergei: "That's it. Patch me through to somebody in the capital."

Ground control: "Which capital? Moscow or Minsk?"

At this point Sergei Krikalev becomes so frustrated and confused, he takes a swig from his bag of Tang only to discover it's actually the ants-reproducing-in-space-slime experiment.

Ground control: "Face it, Sergei, you've been up there for almost a year. A lot of things change."

Sergei: "Some things never change. I've got to be with my wife as quickly as possible!"

Ground control: "Your wife's not speaking to you."

Sergei: "Why not?"

Ground control: "She found out you tried to pick up Canadian astronaut Roberta Bondar last February."

Sergei: "Nothing happened. It was like two spaceships passing in the night."

Ground control: "If it's any consolation, Sergei, Roberta's denying it too."

Sergei: "How did the Soviet hockey team do in Albertville?"

Ground control: "I'm not a sports fan, but let's see . . . I've got the Olympics edition of *Pravda* here . . . Soviet, Soviet, Soviet . . . no, we didn't win a medal."

Sergei: "You're joking. We didn't win a medal in hockey?!"

Ground control: "No. Looks like the Commonwealth took the gold."

Sergei: "The British won a gold in ice hockey! *Pravda* must be playing some kind of communist propaganda trick."

Ground control: "Oh no, Sergei, our newspapers are just like the ones in the West now. They tell the truth."

Sergei: "They do?"

Ground control: "Yeah, did you know that Elvis is still alive?"

Sergei: "Listen, you're making me a little nervous. I better speak to the president."

Ground control: "Okay, I think he's across the hall."

Sergei: "No, no. I want the president, I want to speak to my president of my country of Russia."

Ground control: "Okay, I'll try and reach Yeltsin."

Sergei: "Yeltsin?"

Ground control: "Boris Yeltsin, the president of Russia."

Sergei: "What the hell happened to Mikhail Gorbachev?"

Ground control: "Oh Sergei, you're such a Yakov! Mikhail Gorbachev is a columnist for the Toronto *Star*! . . . Sergei . . . Sergei . . . was that a gun shot?"

Ice Fishing – Guys Watching
Bobbers Not Bob

Most years Lake Erie freezes over in February, bringing onto its slippery surface Roman Catholics and ice fishermen.

By walking on water, Catholics are unsuccessfully attempting to catapult themselves into higher company. By standing in a sub-zero wasteland, hour after hour, staring at holes in the ice, fishermen succeed in making themselves look real damn stupid.

Take my neighbour, John. He's a great guy, large and lovable, with more bad jokes than a stale box of fortune cookies — kind of a Grizzly Adams on a perpetual beer buzz. But when Canada's rocket industry starts searching for a scientist, John will not be on their list of candidates. John's an ice fisherman.

He loves ice fishing. He believes it can provide endless enjoyment for just about any damn fool that happens by. That would be me. I am John's ice-fishing partner. When Canada's rocket industry starts searching for a scientist, I won't be on their list of candidates. I'll be scraping dead minnows off the bottom of my boots or trying to slow the bleeding after removing a non-twist beer cap with my bare right hand in sub-zero weather. I am an ice fisherman.

Ice fishing for yellow perch is big on Sunset Bay, one mile straight out from our front doors.

To be an ice fisherman you need an auger, which is a five-foot-long ice drill — the kind of instrument you imagine the dentist will whip out after he grins and says the words "root canal."

You need a strainer to remove floating ice from the hole you've drilled with the auger. You need hooks and spreaders, tip-ups and tiny poles, a bait bucket with a minnow net, and above all — bobbers.

Bobbers are small red-and-white plastic floats that clip on the top of your line, suspending your baited hook off the lake floor. Most importantly, when the fish bites at the bottom, the bobber bobs atop your little hole in the ice. Bobbers are indispensable. Bobbers are to ice fishermen what the puck is to hockey players, the pulse to a surgeon, the donut to a cop.

Which brings us to method. Ice fishermen spend nine hours a day (or ninety percent of the entire operation) standing stupefied, staring into a dark hole watching red-and-white bobbers not bob. During their entire career, plumbers spend less time looking into dense black holes than an ice fisherman does on a good weekend.

To ease the boredom, John and I have found that if you jump up and down real hard right next to the hole you can make the bobber bob, but after a while the excitement just isn't the same as a real bite.

Which brings us to the other ten percent of the ice fisherman's activity calendar — drinking beer from cans with bare hands and through the ingestion of alcohol into the bloodstream, reducing your corpselike body temperature another twelve degrees.

When a fish does bite and the bobber does bob, you instinctively yank the line to set the hook, then haul the line in, hand over hand until you hoist that perch out of the hole and onto the surface of the ice. I'm sure this happens; John and I have seen others do it many, many times.

Besides watching the bobbers not bob and the holes freeze over every fifteen minutes, John and I have mastered yet another technique of ice fishing — lying to other fishermen about our catch. "We already ate them" is the best we could come up with. "We've been robbed" never worked. We had limited success with "we catch and release."

Some fishermen erect ice-fishing huts out there, for protection. Sure. I've been in one — three holes, a kerosene heater, a food basket, lawn chairs, a battery-operated television set with a ball game blaring. These are not ice-fishing huts, these are Husband Hideaways.

Show me three guys whooping it up in an ice-fishing hut on Sunset Bay, and I'll show you three Wainfleet wives storming around the house and complaining that the garbage never gets taken out.

So ice fishing is like that. A little beer, no bites, more beer, bobbers not bobbing, rebait the hooks — "A beer? Yes, and thanks for asking" — staring into dark holes, freezing your cheeks off, knowing you can never pull a toque down that far on your body.

Ice fishing is a sport the way snoring is a musical genre.

Talking about nothing happening at a snail's pace — ice fishing is like shuffleboard as it's played at Sunset Haven.

The real action happens when offshore wind whips up. Then Miller Time turns to Helicopter Time and fishermen get to see their tax dollars in action as a Canadian Forces helicopter swoops down from Trenton, Ontario, to pluck them from their island of ice, now nearing Dunkirk, New York.

Oh, and there is one more thing. What bodily function is precipitated by cold beer hitting a warm bladder on a chilly winter's

149

day? I'm not sure what your lasting impression of the sport might be, but for me observing forty, and some days sixty, ice fishermen trying to urinate through one-piece snowmobile suits is a sight I won't soon forget. To an ice fisherman, this too is recreation.

The cardinal rule of ice fishing has to do with safety. When the thickness of the ice is exactly equal to the thickness of the head, you're cleared for takeoff. You have found your perfect sport. Enjoy!

Oops, gotta run. John's got the sled ready, and the man gets ugly when I'm late.

Ernie – The Navigational Nerd

Ernie wasn't a bad guy, and under different circumstances we might have gotten along. But on the high seas in a crew of six, you can't pick your friends but you can sure spot your enemies in a hurry.

Ernie and I were opposites — north and south, cat and dog, the Mulroneys and the rest of Canada.

I was on my annual pilgrimage of peril with my friend, Dr. Richard Merrill, who each April tries to introduce me to Davy Jones's locker off the coast of North Carolina. Essentially, we sail his thirty-four-foot Pearson around Cape Hatteras — known as "the graveyard of ships" — just to see if we can make it back to the mainland alive.

Dr. Merrill does it because he is sick, a sadist of the sea, a pathological pirate with a double death wish — his and mine. Why I tag along each year is a matter for me and my analyst.

Last year Dr. Merrill's disappointment at seeing me survive was somewhat abated by my day-long exhibition of projectile vomiting off the bow in six-foot swells and thirty-eight-mile-an-hour winds.

This year the seas seemed right, the wind was at our backs, and the sun shone strong. Then it happened — "Hi, I'm Ernie. I'm your first mate." Whatever Ernie was, I knew right off that he would never be my mate.

When I go sailing, I dress for it: a "Danny Zack's" baseball cap, sunglasses with a safety string, windbreaker, shorts, tennis shoes, an opener, and an ice pack with eight tall Budweisers tied to one ankle.

Ernie was wearing a white Newfoundland fisherman's hood, a white rubber one-piece storm suit with velcro seals at the wrists and ankles, and white knee-high rubber boots.

I looked like I was on vacation. Ernie looked like he was going to mop up Chernobyl. The Marine brushcut that allowed his ears to flair out at the top added military might to his space costume. When I offered him a beer, I expected the Canadian Space Arm to emerge from within and pluck it from me.

"No, thanks, I'll need a clear head. I'm charting our course."

First of all, somebody, probably the bad barber of Greenville, had already cleared that head.

Second, we never charted our course on other trips. I navigated by the sun and the stars. When it was sunny, I insisted on being in sight of land. When the stars came out, I made sure we were tied up at a public dock.

Third, his refusal of a beer verified my first impression. Ernie was going to be as much fun as sharing a compartment with a born-again Christian on a very long train trip.

The first day was a straightaway sail from Bath to Okracoke on the inside of the Outer Banks. It should have been easy, if not pleasant. But Ernie was charting our course as part of a class exercise that would enable him to obtain his Power Squadron Navigational Certificate. Dr. Merrill, who has said certificate, was grading Ernie.

Ernie had charts with matching grids, parallel rulers, triangles, a pen that was resistant to salt water, and a protractor.

He also had a detractor. Me.

I was awash in current checks, stifled by sextants, brow beaten by bearings, and bored stiff by dead reckoning. I wasn't sure where Ernie was steering us, but I knew he was driving me nuts. A hundred yards from the dock, this trip had become my own personal Voyage of the Damned and Ernie was doing a great job of keeping it on course.

In Ernie's navy, I went AWOL. I sat with my back to him playing Jimmy Buffett tapes on a ghetto blaster, counting dolphins and pelicans and empty cans of Budweiser.

My common sense had been chewed up and spit out by the exacting calculations of Ernie's course charting; I was glitch to his computer mind. I gave up. Ernie had won. I could hear the roar of 46,000 nerds at their annual convention in Chicago screaming "Ernie! Ernie!" as he rose to the podium to accept his Navigational Nerd of the Year Award and thank IBM for making him what he was today.

But then it got rather late, too late for the routine sail with a good wind. I noticed off in the distance a marker pass us to port, one we should have taken to starboard. Ernie refused to acknowledge markers; they were for amateurs.

We were lost. Ernie insisted we were on course. "Dead ahead for Okracoke," he announced like a conductor on a train.

Still staring backwards off the stern of the boat, I noticed a needle on the horizon.

"Pass me the binoculars, Ernie," I asked, as he mathematicized furiously over the chart table.

"Won't see anything," he said, passing me the glasses. "Won't be in sight of land for one more hour."

"Then how do you explain that water tower?" I asked, pointing in the opposite direction of our course.

"What water tower?" Ernie barked, like there was a conspiracy under way to remove him from duty.

"The one with Okracoke painted on the side of it," I said with more enthusiasm and enjoyment than I'd had all day.

"What we have here, Captain Merrill," I said, trying unsuccessfully to gloss over the gloating, "is the big Double E. Ernie's Error!"

Dr. Dick was doubled up in laughter at the helm.

Ernie went below and emerged a few minutes later to announce sheepishly he had "forgot to carry a two."

I hate computers, but I suppose they're necessary. I'm not fond of the Ernies of this world, but I reckon they perform a more valuable service than I ever will. But what worries the hell out of me is when they forget to carry that two.

I imagine that when the Russians finally put the finger on the technician responsible for the Chernobyl eruption, he stuck his head through the bars of the train destined for the slag heaps of Siberia and yelled back at the smouldering hole in the ground: "I just forgot to carry a two!" Geez, I hate when that happens!

The Day the Tattoo Man
Took His T-Shirt Off

I am almost certain the story I am about to tell you happened pretty much as it is written. The details are as indelibly etched in my mind as the blue ink of a "Mom" tattoo on the right forearm of a career navy man.

The problem is that the mind was missing on three of its six cylinders the day the Tattoo Man took off his T-shirt.

It was a hot summer morning about fifteen years ago, hot and dank, and the only relief from the sun was the shadow cast by the massive water tower lettered "Beamish Park — Welland, Ontario."

It would have been a routine Sunday morning fastball practice except that the whole team came straight from the catcher's wedding which had started the night before. Fifteen players sharing the same hangover booted grounders, played pop flies off their foreheads, and put their hands over their ears with each new crack of the bat.

155

From third base Howie Doan (Not bad, yourself?) actually coc-cobutted a ball to first base to beat the runner by a full stride. We were a pretty fair fastball team, at our best when we were fighting amongst ourselves and taping over the sponsor's name with masking tape to extract a more equitable pecuniary arrangement (i.e., beer and pizza).

We were C & R Sports, named appropriately after our sponsors Chilly and Rollie, who owned a cubbyhole sporting goods store next to the Rex Hotel on King Street in Welland.

The location was critical. We could buy our cups at C & R Sports, then get well into our cups at the Rex. It was the first really successful attempt at one-stop shopping.

Besides great pitching from Francescutti and Stouck and a vacuum cleaner in centre field by the name of Hank Fraser, we had Ginzy.

Every team should be so lucky as to have a Ginzy. If the world today had travelling Ginzys, most current wars would have to be called on account of laughter.

Ginzy, still the funniest man ever to work a taproom, had one rule: No humour is so low that you can't stoop down, pick it up, and still get a laugh.

The day Ginzy brought the Tattoo Man to practice, the team was in trouble. Besides a K-Mart cart full of aspirin and a bucket each of frothing Alka Seltzer, we needed a win . . . bad. We had a slippery hold on second place and the fall was looming large — playoff time. We were fading faster than the summer sun.

Ginzy was our manager. What Ginzy knew about baseball could be, and in fact was, written on the cuff of his C & R jersey. But what Ginzy knew about human nature and the power of laughter, universities are just now learning.

"Take it off!" Ginzy told the Tattoo Man, who mumbled something negative and stood by the bench as we all crowded around him, his T-shirt still tucked in.

Even with his T-shirt on, the guy was a walking cartoon strip. When he flexed his right arm, Popeye on his biceps punched Olive Oyl, who was perched on his forearm. When he flexed his left arm, Mom kind of caressed Karen but the arrow through the heart that encased Karen had been turned into an X. As if to disclaim his hate for all women, Mom had been circled with a heart a second time in red.

"Take if off," said Ginzy a second time, but the Tattoo Man budged not a bit. A lifelong sailor, he had so many ports-of-call tattooed up and down his arm it looked like the Canadian Navy was using him as a back-up set of files in case of fire at headquarters in Halifax.

"Take if off," said Ginzy again, but this time he whispered something in the guy's ear. I can only imagine that Ginzy offered to pay for a four-coloured bald eagle swallowing a two-foot cobra that spelled out *Sex* across his shoulders.

Anyway, off came the T-shirt, and the Tattoo Man stood before us, naked to the waist.

The first man that saw it fell off the end of the bench. The rest of us followed in twos and threes, and at least one guy was dramatically sick from laughing. The Tattoo Man was kind of the neutron bomb of humour; he slayed people but left the ball-park intact.

The Tattoo Man was a hairy man, his chest and torso covered in a thatch of black wool that ended only at the shaving mark just below his Adam's apple.

With one outstanding exception: a clean, bare, two-inch strip across his chest that he shaved each and every day.

This clean-shaven strip stretched the width of his chest, from one nipple to the other and at one end . . . here it comes . . . at the one end was the perfect tattoo of a man pushing a lawn mower.

If you see the Tattoo Man you'll know it's all true. The chest cartoon of the guy pushing a lawn mower was his idea. The tattoo of the golfer putting into his navel? That was mine.

Ginzy and the Tattoo Man gave C & R Sports the lift we needed to go on and win it all that year.

I saw Ginzy recently, for the first time in years. I was sitting at the bar in a tavern in Welland and Ginzy walked in with his slo-pitch team. When he spotted me he grabbed the very large woman in a baseball uniform nearest him, put her in a headlock, and wrestled her to the floor and pinned her for the count of three.

Then he strutted around the bar with his arms in the air, acknowledging the applause.

Guys! You might as well love 'em, because there's no use trying to shame 'em.

Algin, I Almost Forgot
Why I Loved You

The Blue Star Restaurant in Welland is an ambrosial anachronism, a pre-fern-era, booth-and-swivel-stool restaurant that's a favourite of those who like large amounts of good food at very small prices.

Until a few weeks ago, it was a favourite haunt of mine as well.

I eat only soup at lunch, and in the rush of running errands, I often drop into the Blue Star for a quick bowl which costs one dollar, and you can even find beef in the beef barley soup.

On this particular day, I ran into Algin, a guy I know from my childhood days in Dain City. Algin was sitting at a booth by himself surrounded by enough food to feed a touring polka band.

I remember Malcolm Hilton telling me about the time the Hilton boys took Algin to the Buffalo Zoo because he'd never seen a wild animal.

Returning, the Canada Customs officer began questioning Algin, who was in the back seat. Twice, the Hiltons tried to intervene and twice the officer told them to be quiet and let Algin answer for himself.

Officer: "Where do you live?"
Algin: "Right next door to Taggart's."
Officer: "Where?"
Algin: "Taggart's! Three doors down from the Welland Drive-in."
Officer: "Whatteryou, a wise guy?"
Algin: "No, I'm retarded."
Officer: "That's it . . . pull over."

Then the whole thing happened all over again inside. Suddenly, it dawned on somebody doing the interrogating that Algin was telling the truth. You see, Algin was retarded. (Today, however, he's just mentally handicapped.)

They apologized. Algin's lasting impression of Canada Customs officials is that you have to repeat things very, very slowly before they understand.

Algin is not the smartest guy in the world, but Dain City loves him because he's honest and hardworking and it seems every time he bends down to help somebody, life bites him in the ass.

People, particularly those who are supposed to take care of Algin, keep dying on him all the time.

So Algin is packing away food like it's some kind of pre-hibernation ritual when he waves me over to the booth. At least, I think he beckoned me over but now that I think back on it, he may have been ordering another hot hamburger plate.

So I sat at the booth and by stacking cups on bowls and bowls on plates, I managed to find enough room for my bowl of soup.

We talked about old times, Doris Evens General Store and his buddy Sid Hilton, the first of a long line of friends and guardians Algin has lost along the way. Algin is as happy as ever, even though some cretin stole his bicycle the week before and now he has to walk from Dain City if he wants to come into town.

He wasn't mad, he was curious: "Why'd somebody take a bike like that? I'm the only one who can fix it." I wished I'd had an answer for him.

Lunch went on like that. We talked and Algin polished off the feast with pie and coffee, except that when he saw me savouring the soup he reckoned it must be pretty good, so he had a bowl of that too — after the pie and coffee.

As Algin worked a toothpick to shreds, I waited for a distracting moment, then deftly slid his bill to my side of the table, coupled it with mine, and stood up to leave.

Distracted? I almost had to shake Algin's shoulder to say goodbye to him, because the waitress was delivering food to the booth beside us and Algin was examining every plate. I don't know how this happened, but apparently there were items being served to others that Algin hadn't yet tried that day.

As I pulled a clip of bills from my jeans, I glanced at the bill. Only somebody who has eaten at the Blue Star could appreciate what a job Algin had done running up a $14.50 tab at lunch.

"Say," he says, turning casually from the fresh supplies just delivered at the next table, "you couldn't loan me five bucks, could ya?"

He caught me with a twenty, a ten, and a five.

It's hard to say you don't have it when both of you are staring right at it.

Caught cash in hand, this was one of those moments of truth I'd have rather avoided with a once-over-lightly sprinkling of a little b.s. But you don't fool Algin easily. I mean the Canada Customs guys even had badges and uniforms and they couldn't put one past him.

"Well listen, Algin," I stammered, squirming a bit with awkwardness, "if it's about your lunch tab, I'm paying for that anyway."

161

"Oh I know that," he says with a smile, "I seen ya pick up the bill . . . no, I was just wondering if you'd loan me five bucks."

It was interesting to me how Algin was able to focus on these two events so clearly as to not see any complicated, off-setting link between them. One was a gift he had not asked for; the other was a business transaction he was not about to back away from.

Which is why I'm still steamed at the management of the Blue Star Restaurant in Welland, Ontario.

If you guys, John and Brian I believe it is, if you guys can't serve me a bowl of soup without it costing me $22.80 including tip, then I think you ought to find another line of work.

And Algin, thank you. I almost forgot why I loved you.

V

March 1994 – The Greatest
Month of My Life!

After Dan Quayle left office — Dan Quayle, the former vice-president of the United States of America, who used to frequent Dairy Queen because, as he once explained, they shared the same initials; Dan Quayle who said he could sum up in one word the key to being a good vice-president "and that one word is *to be prepared*"; Dan Quayle who, while campaigning for former President George Bush, once thumped the podium and bellowed: "This president is going to lead us out of this recovery! It will happen!"; Dan Quayle who still strikes a James Dean pose in a poster on my wall — leather jacket, jeans, dangling cigarette over the caption: "Rebel without a Clue"; Dan Quayle who returned from a fact-finding visit to the site of the 1989 San Francisco earthquake to tell a press conference: "The loss of life is irreplaceable" — after Dan Quayle left office, I felt the loss of honest and unintentional humour was irreplaceable.

After Brian Mulroney left office — as an entire nation struggled to express its feelings through the deep blur of a Champagne hangover; as Lyin' Brian, who said history would show him to be a great leader, which caused concerned citizens to begin a search for Canadian historians who were actually paying attention during the 1980s; Brian who said a final farewell to all of us by shooting two wild Russian boars, as Mila offered to sell us back the wallpaper we'd bought her as a housewarming gift — after Brian Mulroney left office, I felt the loss of arrogant and unintentional humour was irreplaceable.

And for a while it was. But then along came the month of March '94 and humourists, cartoonists, and people who make a living by operating polygraphs were back in business once more.

In the month of March, the God of Irony reared its oddball head and got it stuck in a hair dryer for thirty-one days.

March began prophetically enough when a man from Massachusetts, afraid of incurring a heart attack from shovelling snow, hired a guy to plough his driveway. The man was promptly run over by the snowplough and killed in his own driveway.

In March we still had the ass-ends of Lorena Bobbitt, Michael Jackson, and Tonya Harding to kick around. The media circled them in a furious kind of feeding frenzy, like piranha swimming just below the surface of John Wayne's waterbed.

It was a guaranteed scandal every second day or your money back month of the year, a multi-media puppet show starring Kukla, Michael, and Tonya.

And all the lies, the platitudes, and the payoffs turned most North Americans into cringing cynics. But not me. I believed each and every one of them.

I believed Michael Jackson when he swore he was only conducting innocent sleep-overs with young boys, and I believed his lawyer when he claimed the speculated $10 million payoff in no way indicated guilt on the part of the rock star.

I believed Michael's explanation, on the *Oprah Winfrey Show*, that he suffers from a very rare ailment which strikes less than one percent of American males. It's called the Wood-Herman Syndrome.

In the syndrome's later stages, its victims wear military uniforms and keep company with chimpanzees, gradually beginning to look like Natalie Wood and act like Peewee Herman.

I believed John Wayne Bobbitt when he swore he didn't rape his wife. And I believed Lorena Bobbitt when she swore he did. (But honestly, I couldn't believe a jury would acquit anybody of either sex for dismembering another person. Much like the Rodney King and Menendez brothers trials, I just assumed a jury of twelve house pets could find somebody here guilty of something.)

I think I would have opted for a kind of saw-off decision in the Bobbitt case. Put Lorena in jail on a day-to-day basis. The scales of justice dictate fair is fair, so she would get off once he does.

And I believed Tonya Harding when she said she was shocked to learn the details of the plot to injure Nancy Kerrigan.

Tonya, we were all shocked. An estranged-now-reconciled ex-husband, a bodyguard, a hit man, a getaway driver, and $6,000 in cash — and they couldn't manage to kneecap a woman wearing figure skates and a tutu? Shocked! Shocked! Shocked!

Actually, it was a bigger shock for me to learn that these were not the same guys who bombed the World Trade Center in New York, the ones who went back to the rent-a-car agency to try and get their deposit back on the van they used to blow this place up.

I believe Tonya Harding had no clue as to what was going on, mainly because neither did the four guys they convicted in the case.

And who can forget that touching moment at the Olympics in Lillehammer, Norway, when Tonya landed that triple axel, the crowd roared, and the judges thrust their cards in the air: 5.7, 5.8, 5.7, 5.8, 5.9, 10 to 20!

And who can ever forget the great quote from a true champion when Tonya told the media: "A gold medal is what I've worked for all my life. It's the single most sacred prize of my career. And if I win the gold medal the first thing I'm going to do when I get it home is have it bronzed!"

(Okay, okay, so I made that one up. But all the rest is true.)

Yes, I may be the only one, but I still believe in sports, justice, and the American way. I also, however, believe that if people were struck down dead for lying while holding a Bible in their hands, the world's population problem would pretty much be solved.

All three scandals were quietly dismissed from continual front-page appearances when Juan Antonio Samaranch officially declared the start of the XVII Olympic Winter Games, thus proving Lillehammer was a place in Norway and not merely John Wayne Bobbitt's new nickname.

Meanwhile, back in the United States, the Pentagon announced they were refitting U.S. Air Force bombers with new cooling systems that did not expel chlorofluorocarbons into the atmosphere. The nuclear payload those planes deliver still has the capability of moving Moscow into the southern wine-growing area of France, but this new environmental system will ensure that the ozone layer will remain untouched. Yes, in March 1994 the world breathed a sigh of relief with the introduction of environmentally friendly nuclear weapons.

In Sun Valley, Idaho, the home of Olympic skier Picabo Street, the local hospital named their new intensive care unit after the town's favourite daughter. Henceforth, and with a straight face, the new annex will be called Picabo I.C.U.

In Toronto, much to her amazement, a professional fragrance demonstrator was fired by Calvin Klein Canada because, according to the company, she "smelled bad." This was like a runway model being let go for slouching, but nonetheless it happened.

And also in Toronto the Good, a labourer with the Toronto Transit Commission was reinstated after being fired for having sex with a prostitute in an alleyway off King Street while on the job. (For the record, both of them were on the job.) The incident would have gone unnoticed, except the labourer refused to pay the prostitute her $20 fee and she complained to TTC brass. And you really can't blame her. I mean if you show up at a TTC turnstile with no money, they're not going to let you ride for free either. In arbitration, the union lawyer won the man his job back by successfully arguing that while dismissal was too severe, *discipline* was appropriate. I'm no expert in these kind of things but if there's *discipline* involved, isn't that an extra $20?

At this point, I thought March had pretty much hit its maximum humour limit when I came across the story of Eid Saleh Jahaleen of Amman, Jordan. As a devout member of a hardline terrorist group, Eid entered the Salwa Theatre in the city of Zarqua, Jordan, and planted a homemade bomb under his seat as part of an ongoing campaign against the decadence and immorality of modern society. Eid set the timer on the bomb to go off in forty-five minutes and then he . . . he . . . he got a little distracted by the porno flick playing on the screen. In fact, he got a lot distracted — forty-five minutes' worth, to be precise. That's right. Of all the legs that were being thrust upward in that theatre, two of them used to belong to Eid.

Eid, now legless, told police he planted the bomb in protest of lewd and pornographic films in today's society.

And just when I thought I had heard the strangest of stories told in March, along came a dog named Lucky.

Tim Laing, my good friend and *Land of the Loony* radio partner, faxed me a clipping from the *Europa Times* newspaper in which dog trainer Ernst Gerber declared at a news conference: "We will not have to put him down. Lucky is basically a damn good guide-dog. He just needs a little brush-up on some elementary skills, that's all."

Gerber admitted to the press conference that Lucky, a German shepherd guide-dog for the blind, had so far been responsible for the deaths of all four of his previous owners. Said the trainer: "I admit it's not an impressive record on paper." Lucky led his first owner in front of a moving bus, and the second off the end of a pier. He actually pushed his third owner off a railway platform just as the Cologne-to-Frankfurt express was approaching, and he

walked his fourth owner into heavy traffic, before abandoning him and running away to safety. (Lucky may be quite a klutz, but at least he's not stupid!)

Asked if Lucky's fifth owner would be told about his previous record, Gerber replied: "No. It would make them nervous, and that would make Lucky nervous. And when Lucky gets nervous, he's liable to do something silly."

Yeah, like push a busload of Portuguese tourists off a road in the German Alps. I mean really, what more harm could he do?

Never mind being a damn good guide-dog. I think what *Lucky* needs is a damn good guide-dog.

And wouldn't Lucky make a great guide dog for Eid? All Lucky has to do is learn to sniff out bombs and someday he could quite literally save Eid's ass, which is just about all that's left of the poor man.

On the last day of March, in casual conversation, somebody asked me: "Do you think the NDP could get back into power in Ontario?"

My first inclination was to laugh hysterically and try to keep from falling, but then I reflected back on the month for a moment and replied quite honestly: "Stranger things have happened, that's for sure." March 1994, the greatest month a humorist could ever have.